TRUCK BEDS

Kevin Tetz

HOW TO INSTALL, RESTORE, & MODIFY

CarTech®

CarTech®

CarTech®, Inc.
6118 Main Street
North Branch, MN 55056
Phone: 651-277-1200 or 800-551-4754
Fax: 651-277-1203
www.cartechbooks.com

Edit by Wes Eisenschenk
Layout by Connie DeFlorin

ISBN 978-1-61325-765-4
Item No. SA535

Library of Congress Cataloging-in-Publication Data Available

Written, edited, and designed in the U.S.A.
Printed in China
10 9 8 7 6 5 4 3 2 1

All photos are courtesy of Kevin Tetz unless otherwise noted.

DISTRIBUTION BY:

Europe
PGUK
63 Hatton Garden
London EC1N 8LE, England
Phone: 020 7061 1980 • Fax: 020 7242 3725
www.pguk.co.uk

Australia
Renniks Publications Ltd.
3/37-39 Green Street
Banksmeadow, NSW 2109, Australia
Phone: 2 9695 7055 • Fax: 2 9695 7355
www.renniks.com

Canada
Login Canada
300 Saulteaux Crescent
Winnipeg, MB, R3J 3T2 Canada
Phone: 800 665 1148 • Fax: 800 665 0103
www.lb.ca

TABLE OF CONTENTS

Dedication 4

Introduction 4

Chapter 1: Traditional Bed Floor Restoration 5
- Bed Floor Candidates 6
- "Over" Restoration 7
- Analyzing and Preparing Bed Boards 10
- Stripping Wood Mechanically 12
- Restoring Original Painted Bed Strips 15

Chapter 2: Bed Floor Replacement 17
- Organizing the Bed Kit 18
- New Hardware 21
- Bed Floor Removal 23
- Test-Fitting 24
- Cam Bolts and Hidden Fasteners 27
- Truck Bed Kit Installation 27
- Making Your Own Bed Boards 47

Chapter 3: Custom Wood Floor Options 55
- Craftsmanship Meets Computer-Controlled Automation 60
- Finish Coatings and Options 64
- Immortalizing a Memory 66

Chapter 4: Aluminum Bed Floors 69
- Aluminum Bed Floor in a Traditional Restoration Project 73

Chapter 5: Wood Floors for Modern Trucks 77
- CAD Modeling and the Modern Age of Design 79
- SUVs with Truck Beds 86

Chapter 6: Creating the Illusion of Age 88
- Creating Patina on New Wood 90
- Personalizing Your Patina 92
- Driftwood 93
- Water-Based and Oil-Based Clear Coatings 94

DEDICATION

This book is dedicated to my grandfather Andrew Tetz, who made his living with wood and showed me that hard work is its own reward.

INTRODUCTION

The bed floor has more surface area than any other location on a truck, which makes it the focal point. The hood may be the most visible panel on most vehicles, but the focus is on the bed in my trucks. Trucks were designed to be workhorses that fulfilled a single purpose: to haul a load. In today's high-tech trucks, this morphed into hauling loads in extreme comfort.

A 1918 Packard advertisement stated that you could "eliminate the need for rail transport with its hauling capacity!" Rail transport was the norm, and small-load transportation vehicles were a new idea. Today, it is called a "disruptor" in the industry. Although it happens much more frequently today, a paradigm shift such as going from rail transport to a single truck and all the versatility it offered was truly a game changer.

It's amazing to think about the concept of a personal work vehicle being something new. For most of us, trucks have always been available in one form or another. However, it's a relatively new concept historically speaking, and trucks have come a long way in the past 100-or-so years.

In the mid-1950s, trucks were finally recognized as passenger vehicles that could benefit from options such as radios, ashtrays, and upholstery. Fast-forward to today, and the pickup truck is much more widely used for basic personal transportation than it is used as a workhorse, and the level of luxury options are as plentiful as any high-end sedan.

Full disclosure: I own a late-model Ram truck that I'm hesitant to use to set a load in the bed without placing cardboard or a blanket around the load so that the paint doesn't get scratched. The forefathers of the initial truck designs are laughing at me, I know. However, the fact that consumer needs have changed led to changes in truck use and truck beds along with them.

Wood bed floors are long gone, but millions of trucks still have them in service, and millions more are being preserved, restored, or replaced. Vintage wood floors were poorly prepared by the factory when they were installed. The wood was primarily pine, but some deviations were made, depending on availability at the time of manufacturing.

In Ford Motor Company's early days, it had several massive sawmills and milled its own wood from privately held groves of oak and pine in Michigan's upper peninsula, manufacturing wheels, floors, and framework. Almost none of the manufacturers sealed the boards on assembly, and being unfinished certainly contributes not only to the character of the vintage wood but also to the many failed and rotten floors in vintage trucks.

TRUCK BEDS How to Install, Restore, and Modify

CHAPTER 1

TRADITIONAL BED FLOOR RESTORATION

This truck, which is barely visible, has been long forgotten, and the bed floor is completely missing. Sadly, this truck and the bed floor have been nearly reclaimed by nature and stand no chance of restoration.

We would like our classic vehicles to last forever, but the truth is that they won't. We maintain them and hope they'll survive long enough for the next caretaker. This can include a regular cleaning or even a full restoration of the original parts and pieces. Even a decent-condition Chevrolet Advance Design truck from 1947 to 1953 sitting in the woods brings several thousand dollars these days—even if it's incomplete.

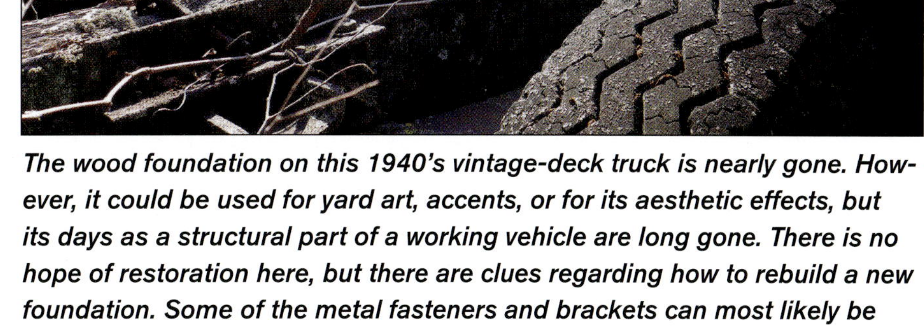

The wood foundation on this 1940's vintage-deck truck is nearly gone. However, it could be used for yard art, accents, or for its aesthetic effects, but its days as a structural part of a working vehicle are long gone. There is no hope of restoration here, but there are clues regarding how to rebuild a new foundation. Some of the metal fasteners and brackets can most likely be reused, but the wood is too far gone.

Stories are common of people saying that they will restore the truck someday but let the vehicle sit untended and deteriorating for generations. That was the case for this workhorse 3100-series truck that was left in a field in middle Tennessee for many years.

Although enough aftermarket manufacturers and parts are available for these trucks to bring them back from almost any state of deterioration, this truck deteriorated a little too long, and the owner still won't sell it and was reluctant to allow me to take photos.

Bed Floor Candidates

This F-1 truck has been changed very little from its original form (other than aftermarket wheels and a bad paint and body job). Someone tried to make his or her own bed floor as a replacement but stopped about 70 percent through the project. Gravity now holds the boards in place, and they were never finished, which led to deep cracks in the planks from moisture penetration and expansion and contraction with various temperature cycles. This may be fine for a limited-use farm truck or an ongoing project where you haven't gotten to the bed parts yet, but it's not ready for either world. It fails at being both a restored showpiece and a nice resto-mod. Although, the bones are good in this truck.

If you're looking for a project vehicle, don't let a bed floor such as this discourage you from buying it. This book guides you through several great ways to install a pre-manufactured kit or even cut your own boards that properly fit inside any bed framework. Make sure that you perform a thorough inspection.

The bed has been replaced with homemade boards that were laid into the bed frame without any retaining strips. The sound that this truck makes while driving over bumps or railroad tracks must be incredible. Although this makeshift bed can support a load, its potential has not been maximized. The tailgate hinge shows clues of the original color of the truck and also shows that some attention needs to be paid to the metal, which needs integrity to support the wood floor.

This shows the effect of leaving wood unfinished, as there are several large fractures in the boards. Although damage such as this can be glued and clamped, the boards that have deteriorated may need to be replaced. Pay close attention to the spacing between the boards. Most bed strips need at least 1/2 inch between the boards. This allows the wood to expand and contract depending on the temperature. It also allows the corners of the metal strips to sit in the groove of the board for stability and strength. These boards are probably too close together, so even these temporary boards need to be trimmed.

TRUCK BEDS How to Install, Restore, and Modify

There are signs of rust that need to be investigated further on this example, but it's still a great foundation to work on, even if you have a little metalwork to do before the woodwork on the bed.

"Over" Restoration

We remember our past romantically. This means that we recall the past better than it actually was: cars were faster, paint jobs were smoother, beer was colder, and life was better. The tendency to "over-restore" vehicles has taken over the traditional restoration models of the past, where a vehicle may have been restored to the standard that it was produced. Today, the tendency is to restore to today's high standard of finish quality and attention to detail.

The 1951 Chevrolet restored by Randy Borcherding and his team at Painthouse in Texas is a perfect example. The panels are file-fit, upholstery is better than new, chrome plating is show quality, and the options on the truck have been enhanced and embellished. In truth, this is a stunning museum piece and a vehicle that will seldom be driven unless it's a very special occasion. The owner wanted finesse and nostalgia in one package, and the build quality is amazing. The cost of a restoration such as this can end up in six figures, depending on the condition and degree of detail.

The overall effect is that we're reminded of the classic vehicle, but we're rewarded with current show-quality craftsmanship. All the classic earmarks of an original truck are in this wonderful example, and it's been elevated to custom show status in the best possible way.

This 1951 Advance Design Chevrolet truck has been beautifully restored by Painthouse in Cypress, Texas. Some liberties were taken in the restoration with period-correct details, such as white-wall tires, chrome accents, the rain visor, and dual chrome mirrors. All of which may have been an option but were not standard equipment. Every nut and bolt on this truck has been removed, refurbished, finished, and reassembled in a far more precise way than the factory did. Technically, this is an over-restoration, but it shows beautifully and was exactly what the client wanted. (Photo Courtesy Randy Borcherding)

The original pine or maple bed floor was replaced with an oak kit from an aftermarket manufacturer. The bed boards were beautifully refinished with stain and polyurethane, and new polished stainless-steel bed strips and hardware replaced the original painted carbon steel. It is a nod to the original but is a modern and attractive upgrade.

This 1950 Chevrolet truck was previously restored but is in need of a second restoration. It's hard to believe that this vehicle is more than 70 years old. Auto body and painting technology has improved, and materials are much higher quality today. Although this truck looks solid and is complete, it shows wear, age, and neglect. While it runs great, doesn't burn oil, and only requires a tune-up mechanically, the paint is faded and needs to be redone.

Although this bed floor was previously replaced, it shows signs of wear, and the finish is delaminating. However, this floor can be saved. To remove the old finish, use a chemical stripper, sand, or mechanically strip it off. Then, start over with the raw wood and use a stain and finish coat. To restore this wood floor properly, it must be completely disassembled.

The bed is made from oak and is an aftermarket kit that was created for this truck design. The wood was lightly stained and topcoated with automotive polyurethane satin clear coats that have the same durability and modern chemistry of the painted exterior panels. Selecting the correct wood finish for a bed floor is a decision that needs to be carefully made. The stainless-steel strips are an upgrade but look perfectly vintage with the exposed domes of the carriage bolts and cam-centric mounting bolts in the corners. Custom boltless strips, or a high-gloss wood finish would look out of place on this vehicle.

Millions of trucks have been restored in the 50- to 70-year span since these vehicles were mass produced. Some trucks have been restored several times, depending on their use and the quality of the new components that were used. Finding a truly original vehicle today is quite rare, and there's even a new "barn find" category that is used when an unmolested vintage vehicle is found. This can present its own set of challenges when it comes to properly restoring or even assessing the original condition of the vehicle.

Car shows, cars-and-coffee events, and even museums are often great places to research how things should be repaired and restored.

The subject truck for this book was stumbled upon by my neighbor

The underside shows the retaining bolts and washers that hold everything in place. You can also see that the floor was not properly sealed and finished on the bottom side. This is most likely why the finish on top began flaking off, as moisture penetrated and traveled in the open structure of the wood, getting under the finish and lifting it. Wood is like a sponge. If the structure of the wood is left open, it will absorb, expand, and contract, which can cause the flaking that is seen on the edges of the cured non-flexible finish.

This board came from BedWood and is a beautifully preserved original sideboard from a 1941 Ford F-Series truck. Boards such as this weren't finished at the assembly line, and this one most likely was coated with oil or a permeating material during the course of its life as a work truck. Although the board looks bad right now, the use of oil or a permeating material actually helped preserve the integrity of the wood.

in an industrial park when he bought several vintage trucks at an estate sale. I immediately grabbed my camera and crawled around a 1944 Chevrolet and this once-restored 1951 Chevrolet, making notes and taking shots of the bed floors and the rest of the truck for this book and future reference.

Although these are not professional restorations by any means, each holds a clue to restoring or repairing different situations that you may run into in your restoration. I seldom have the opportunity to start with a factory-original vehicle, and these trucks are much more typical of what you'll find in a new project today. Today's project

vehicles most likely have been completely painted, probably with some degree of rust repair and bodywork done but with older-technology paint and techniques that give it a dated look without the mystique of the original finish.

Analyzing and Preparing Bed Boards

Clean, flat countertops can never be underestimated. My benchtops are lined with thick masking paper from the home center to keep things tidy and to create a surface where I can see everything. Plus, if anything spills, cleanup is easy. Just replace the paper. You'll use up

counter space fast with any project, so plan ahead and get organized before starting the project.

Wood can be challenging to restore, especially if it's original antique wood. A metal fender can always be replaced if it's rusted, bent, or even if I damage it during the restoration process, but wood is much more fragile and sensitive. Restoring original wood requires a plan and a lot of forethought so that you don't make irreparable mistakes.

TRUCK BEDS How to Install, Restore, and Modify

The edges and ends of the board show wear but not rot. Note the groove cut into the rabbet on the side of the board. This is intended to be used to interlock the bed strips to retain the boards and allow for adjustability and expansion.

The bottom side of this board shows more wear than the top. Road debris, gravel, and sand pelted this for decades and wore down the raw wood around the bracing.

Trying the least-aggressive method first is my best advice for cleaning and refinishing wood. This applies to cleaners as well, and I recommend simple soaps, such as dishwashing liquid, that are designed to remove grease but are PH friendly to the wood. Many industrial cleaners are available, and some are very aggressive. Avoid anything with bleach in it because bleach can penetrate the wood fiber and expand and degrade the cellular structure. Simple soaps work well, and using a soft-bristled brush scrubbed gently with the grain of the wood is a non-destructive technique. It is evident quickly if you're doing a good job or if you need to step up to something stronger. Allow time for the wood to dry between sessions so that you can assess the next step while still preserving the shape and integrity of the boards.

The first step to restore this wood is to clean it with a simple soap. Use dishwashing liquid or a cleaner from the home center with a soft-bristled brush to remove the debris. It allows you to get a better look at the wood.

A soft-bristled brush gets into the grain of the wood without damage. The dirt being pulled from the surface can be seen as it is scrubbed in several sessions. If you're pre-cleaning original wood, it's fine to give it a good soaking. However, make sure that it is left in a dry environment for a few days so that the moisture can evaporate before you do any further work or refinishing.

The beautiful grain of the wood is revealed as the decades of dirt get washed out of the wood. Rinse and repeat as many times as necessary (as long as dirt is lifted from the pores of the wood). Two sessions were enough to clean this board. There were no longer any dirty bubbles after rinsing the board for a second time.

Stripping Wood Mechanically

Using rotary tools can remove a lot of material in a hurry from any substrate, especially wood. When restoring vintage wood, preserve as much originality and character as possible while still removing the upper layers of oxidation, staining, and light damage. The restorer tool is a drum sander that has a wide footprint on the surface, variable speed control, and multiple interchangeable drums. For this project, I used a fiber-disc drum because it only removes a small layer of the surface in a very controlled manner. Light and even pressure is important when using this tool and works very well. I like to use this tool on wood because it rotates in one direction and can be directed with the grain of the wood instead of across it. I prefer this tool over a dual-action sander in this application.

Linseed oil is also known as flaxseed oil and is one of the most popular and easy-to-use wood finishes. Linseed oil soaks deep into the wood, protects against scratches and changes in humidity, and brings out

Once the wood has dried overnight (or longer), use a rotary "restorer" tool to resurface the board and remove any remaining embedded dirt and expose a new layer of wood.

　　TRUCK BEDS How to Install, Restore, and Modify

Light pressure and constant movement work well with this tool. It is loaded with 180-grit sandpaper so that only the upper surface of the wood is removed. This reveals a new layer that exposes the grain and character of these boards.

Next, sand with a short-stroke dual-action sander to level the surface and prepare for the finish coats. This sander orbits in a very tight circle (3/32 inch) and is designed for surface preparation on finished automotive coatings. The short stroke minimizes the sanding marks across the grain and allows us to refine the surface.

Boiled linseed oil has been a popular wood coating for many years. It is easy to apply and shows the character of the wood with a single coating. If a strictly traditional restoration is performed, no stain is applied because the factory applied none during the assembly process in 1941. Linseed oil absorbs into the wood for some degree of moisture resistance and retains the look of unfinished wood.

Boiled linseed oil is applied by simply wiping the oil onto the board and working it into the surface with a soft towel or lambswool. Follow each application with a dry rag to remove any oil pooling. For a bed floor, apply at least three coats and wait a few hours between each application.

You can see where the wood was covered by the metal bed, but the board has great integrity and character. A whole bed floor like this is a beautiful focal point of any restored truck.

the grain of the wood. This product is available at most hardware stores and is nontoxic. The flax plants have been cultivated for textile, seeds, and oils for over 20,000 years, and they provide a very inexpensive and beautiful finish to any wood surface. Linseed oil quickly penetrates the surface of the wood and dives into the fiber, creating a water-resistant coating that repels moisture. Application is simple, and it can even be applied over some stains if you want a darker tone. I wanted the natural beauty of this original wood to come through and still show the character of some of the deep wounds that it's suffered over its life.

Restoring Original Painted Bed Strips

There's nothing nicer than polished stainless-steel bed strips in a classic truck. Frankly, there's not an easier retaining strip to maintain, either. However, if you're working for a client who wants a traditional, original look (or if you're restoring a truck to look the way it was from the factory), you'll need to restore or replace the steel painted bed strips.

Grinding off paint, removing rust, and using plastic fillers and conventional autobody techniques can restore any metal finish, but due to the detail and complex shape of these strips, it's very time-consuming. The juice may not be worth the squeeze. Aftermarket strips are inexpensive and available, but they require the refinishing process to be done properly. You can even paint stainless-steel strips if you want a substrate that will never rust and a traditional look, but typically, if the original carbon steel parts and hardware are properly prepped, the result will be a durable and long-lasting finish.

Use professional-quality materials and not just any old spray can, especially if you want durability. Recently, the introduction of catalyzed spray cans has given non-painters and non-trained enthusiasts the ability to create professional results with rattle-can techniques. The rules still apply, such as those for proper surface prep, paying attention to between-coat drying times, and making a clean and safe environment in which to spray toxic chemicals. Anyone can expertly apply the simple steps that I use with this Eastwood setup and achieve professional-quality results without an expensive compressor and spray-gun setup. New technology provides more possibilities and the potential for incredible results.

Restoring a truck floor doesn't need to be expensive. The wonderful array of products and parts that are available can be overwhelming. Most restorations come down to the trade-off of time and money. Doing it yourself and spending more time or paying someone else a lot of

The metal retaining strips can be damaged in a bed floor. These metal strips were bent and rusty. Although the metal retaining strips and hardware could have been restored, they were recycled because new aftermarket replacements fit well and are relatively inexpensive.

This strip is worthy of restoration. Most people opt for a new kit with hardware because they're relatively inexpensive. However, if you are a diehard restoration buff, anything is possible. Start with a stripping disc on a rotary tool to strip paint and any surface rust from the metal.

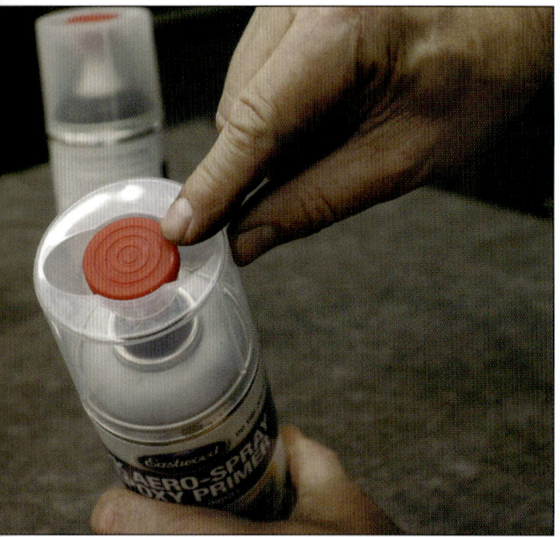

Eastwood has a two-part paint system that puts professional-grade paint into a spray can. Hitting the button on the valve at the bottom of the can releases the hardener into the paint, which gives a crosslinked material that is much stronger than a typical rattle can. Read and follow the instructions. They're very simple but very important to understand.

money instead of investing time is up to you. Personally, I enjoy the process of restoration as much as seeing the results.

The investment and strategy in building or restoring your truck floor is your decision, and there's never been a better time to make whatever decision is right for you and your project.

Long-lasting paint is needed on this part. An epoxy primer bonds to the metal very well and serves as a great undercoat for any paint. After a coat of epoxy, let it flash off for 15 to 20 minutes.

Satin black paint provides an original look and is a very forgiving finish. It won't reflect dust in the surface with the satin sheen. This coating is easily done in a home workshop (especially with the Eastwood rattle-can catalyzed paint system), and the benefit is a long lasting and very durable coating. As with any paint (especially with catalyzed paint systems), wear proper personal protective equipment to protect your eyes and respiratory system. Also, cover up any tools or items to keep them clean from overspray. A well-ventilated area is important too. Be safe.

CHAPTER 2

Bed Floor Replacement

Chevrolet was slow to change from the traditional wood floor to a stamped-steel floor in its full-size trucks. Examples are known up to 1987, and there's something cool and nostalgic about a wood bed floor, even though replacement can seem like an intimidating restoration project. LMC Truck makes several versions of these replacements. The company also offers bed strips, hardware kits, and even stainless-steel and polished versions of each.

This is an original, long-wheelbase 1966 Chevrolet C-10 that was ordered with a 283-ci engine, 3-speed manual transmission, AM radio, windshield washers, chrome bumpers, and two-tone paint with side moldings. It served as a farm truck for several years and was relegated to hauling wood and mulch for 26 years, being garaged the whole time. Rust is minimal, and the overall condition is excellent, except for the bed floor. This truck has been owned by the same family since it was new. So, sentimental value and its history make it a worthy candidate for a new bed floor.

Many options are available for those who want to replace the bed floor of a vintage truck, and many vendors offer replacement kits. A high-quality floor kit is designed to fit perfectly and replace the original floor with minimal

The bed floorboards are shot. The original pine wood provided nearly 60 years of use but is now rotting, full of holes, and unsafe for hauling. The steel retaining strips are still intact, but some are bent and dented, and most of the carriage-bolt fasteners are frozen with rust. It's time for a replacement.

adjustments or modifications. This book shows installation techniques and how to fit a new system into your truck. Refinishing techniques are also shown to keep your new boards looking great for decades.

Some enthusiasts with woodworking skills choose to make their own boards, and although this can be time consuming, it can save money and be a personal approach. BedWood in Hopkinsville, Kentucky, mills its own floor systems from rough-cut lumber that is sourced in a variety of different woods, which provides many options to replace or restyle truck bed floors.

Organizing the Bed Kit

After unpacking and inspecting the wood kit, look closely at all of the boards and lay them out in a well-lit area. Inspect the boards for damage, splits, and (most importantly) the way the grain shows on the face side of the boards. Depending on the degree of a split, these can be repaired by gluing and clamping, but severe splits should be documented and possibly returned to the manufacturer for replacement.

One of the beautiful things about natural wood is its imperfection, but no one wants unnatural defects. Each board has character, and the way that the boards are arranged has an effect on the overall

This is the new oak wood kit from LMC Truck. It was precision cut with beautiful exposed grain, and the oak will last longer than the original pine. Most manufacturers provide options as to the type of wood. Then, you can select the stain and finish.

   TRUCK BEDS How to Install, Restore, and Modify

To be faithful with how this truck was manufactured, either the original bed strips and hardware or replacement steel strips and bolts can be used. Since some of the strips were rusted through and dented, replacements were needed, and I opted for the upgraded polished stainless-steel strips. They came polished from the manufacturer, were very accurate to the original tooling, and provided an original yet custom touch to the bed floor.

appearance. Arrange the boards so that they look balanced in design and color, with the grain flowing and matching from board to board. This is a fun way to have a hand in the appearance of your floor and to make sure that it appears symmetrical and purposeful. Most wood kits have hardware and bed strips included. This one from LMC Truck did, and there was the option of steel or stainless strips as well as exposed or hidden fasteners.

Keep track of how the original boards were oriented if you can remove them intact. Label them in the order in which they were removed. If they're like the boards for this project (they disintegrate in your hands), make a template, if possible, to keep track of placement. Using the original boards as a template for comparison can help with the installation of the new floor. If a

A stainless-steel bolt kit matches the strips and completes the look of the floor. The carriage bolt heads were polished to a high gloss and came complete with lock washers and nuts. Another benefit of stainless-steel bolts is that they won't rust over time. Traditional carriage bolts are smooth without ID markings on the dome, but they are typically shipped in raw steel and will require painting before installation to prevent corrosion.

The eccentric bolts and washers attach the bed to the truck frame and allow for adjustment of the bed on the chassis. I chose the stainless-steel option. Since this job is easier with the bed off the frame, I pulled the bed off the chassis and then removed all the original hardware.

Take several photos of your bed before you disassemble anything. Do you see how the boards and strips fit under the wheelhouse? This, along with the notes that you take, is your guide to reassembly. Sometimes it can be weeks, months, or even years before you reassemble your new bed. Photos and reference notes come in handy when installing your new wood kit.

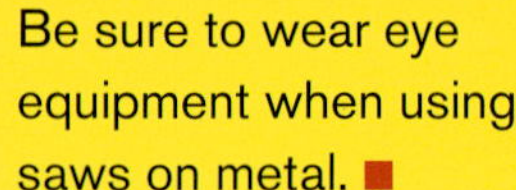

The bed is being removed to provide better access for installation as well as better photos. Start with removing the eccentric bolts at each corner. On this truck, they are rusted solid and cannot be un-bolted. To make the carriage bolts easier to remove, an "X" is cut into the head because the carriage bolts will be replaced.

The head of the bolt has been split four ways. This allows the pieces to be chiseled off and easily removed. Wear eye protection.

long time passes between removal and reinstallation, an organized record of how the boards were originally placed saves you time and frustration. Some full restoration projects take three to five years, and relying on memory for reassembly is not the best practice.

TRUCK BEDS How to Install, Restore, and Modify

New Hardware

Since the entire system, including the mounting hardware, is being replaced for this project, there's no reason to save anything. The bolts were rusted to the point that the nuts couldn't unthread, and it was more important to remove the bed floor efficiently than to try to save the degraded bolts.

Using a cut-off wheel to eliminate the head of each bolt allows them to be driven down from the top instead of pulled up, which would require careful and awkward removal from the bottom side. Removing the bed from the chassis provides complete access, and an engine hoist and bed-lifter system allow this to be done with a single worker.

Using an air hammer with a chisel blade removes a bolt head in seconds, but a sharp hand chisel and big hammer does the job as well.

Removing the bed is usually a job for several friends (one on each corner). However, an engine hoist and a bed-lifter fixture make it a one-man operation. Before you lift too high, make sure that the bed is balanced.

The rest of the carriage bolts are rusted solid as well. If there was no other option, I would soak them in penetrating oil for several days, carefully try to remove them, and save them for reuse. However, bolt kits are relatively inexpensive, so I'm not saving anything, and I'm getting to the mockup process much faster.

     TRUCK BEDS How to Install, Restore, and Modify

You aren't required to remove the bed to replace the floor, but it helps with fastener access. With the bed off, inspect the chassis and read suspension components for wear. You can even refinish the frame rails and freshen things up for rust control. Having the bed on a rolling stand also helps if your shop is small so that the truck can be moved to another location while the bed is being worked on. The stand for this project is from Auto Body Toolmart and can safely hold up to 1,000 pounds. The locking swivel casters

With all of the wood removed, the bed will sit on the cross-sills and not allow proper installation or spacing. The bed boards are 3/4 inch thick, so some 3/4-inch square tubing acts as a perfect spacer to get the bedsides off the braces.

Lay out all of the boards, mocked up the arrangement, and number them in order. Match the grain, and because there are two narrower boards that are directly in the center of the pattern, arrange them the way they will be installed into the bed.

make it easy to move around, and it folds up and hangs on the wall when not in use.

Test-Fitting

Even though most original bed wood was unfinished by the manufacturer, it's not good practice to install unfinished wood in your truck. Being careful not to handle the wood with dirty hands or gloves will save you a lot of cleanup later and will ensure that there aren't adhesion problems with the finish-coats as well. After the location of each board has been decided, number the underside of each board. This provides a roadmap to keep track of the wood pattern that is desired.

Having access to the underside of the bed floor helps with layout and installation. It's also a great way to inspect the cross-braces to determine if they need to be replaced. Several manufacturers have replacement parts available. If you see rust-through or damaged parts, now's the time to reach out to your vender of choice for replacement parts. On the project vehicle, there is surface rust on the cross-braces, but they were all solid and had no

Install the outside and corner boards first. Avoid hitting them directly with a hammer for adjustment because this can bruise the wood and distort the shape. Use a scrap piece of wood between the hammer and bed floor as a drift.

TRUCK BEDS How to Install, Restore, and Modify

The next pieces are not interchangeable with an offset wheel housing and can only be installed one way. After these planks, the orientation of the boards is personal preference or dependent on the orientation of a fuel filler that's mounted flush in the bed floor. (The front and rear sideboards take the place of the 3/4-inch steel spacer at this time.)

Aligning the stainless-steel strips begins with the wheel housing, and the shape of the stamped strips combined with the grooves in the boards are the perfect guide for correct board spacing.

damage. Since this is a mockup and for test-fitting only, clean up the surface rust from the cross-sills and repaint them before installing the new floor.

"Mockup" is a frequently used term used in the automotive custom and restoration world. It falls under the philosophy of "measure twice, cut once." Test-fitting your system provides information regarding what fits and what doesn't—and trust me, there will be plenty that doesn't fit. This is not the fault of the aftermarket manufacturers or even the fault of a 60-plus-year-old vehicle, it's simply a byproduct of marrying older construction and manufacturing standards of newly manufactured parts and pieces. Don't expect everything to just fall into place. Even on the assembly lines, workers had to make adjustments to align panels.

TRUCK BEDS How to Install, Restore, and Modify

The eccentric washers allow for proper alignment of the bed and wood strips with the floor assembled, but they need to be countersunk into the boards for a factory-looking fit. Practice the procedure on a scrap 2x4 before drilling into the boards. A 1-1/2-inch woodworking bit is being used here. It was sunk down 1/8 inch so that the washer fit flush.

Cam Bolts and Hidden Fasteners

A traditional installation uses concentric washers on the top of the boards with bolts extending down to connect the bed to the frame rails. Doing this requires you to create and exact placement of these adjustment points, which can be risky if you have limited equipment and woodworking skills. I practiced on a 2x4 to show you how, but I opted instead to attach from underneath the bed floor and hide these mounting bolts. It makes for a cleaner-looking installation, but it's not accurate for a traditional restoration.

With the cross-sills in place, mark the location from the underside. The domed head of the carriage bolt will lift the board off the sill and will be misaligned if you don't make an adjustment. With the board marked where the head of the bold will be, use a carbide burr to cut a pocket into the bottom of the board where the bolt head will go. This allows the fastener to be hidden without a goofy raised edge on the board.

With the bed floor installed and aligned, mark all of the perimeter holes for drilling. The small carriage bolts in the project kit have a 1/4-inch shank, so I used a 5/16-inch bit, which provides some wiggle room for final assembly. The bed floor has properties of both a floating floor and a fixed floor. It's bolted firmly in place but also needs to flex with the chassis under various driving conditions.

Truck Bed Kit Installation

If you decided to replace the original wood with a kit from an aftermarket vendor, there is a very fulfilling but time-consuming project on your hands. The only other time you'll use both woodworking and metalworking skills on a vehicle is with a pre-1935 car or truck because manufacturers stopped using wood reinforcements on car and truck bodies after that time. It's refreshing that a computer is not necessary for either skill, and this type of project can be therapeutic.

At some point, I'll completely restore this project 1966 Chevrolet C10, but for now, I'll just enjoy a beautiful bed floor in the back. Believe it or not, the paint can be revived to a high gloss, even with the current state of faded oxidation on the surface.

I enjoy working by myself, but it presents its own challenges. If I had a helper, I could lift up on these

Using the eccentric washer, mark a location for the carriage bolt, which on the actual bed board is marked from the bottom.

Drill a 3/8-inch hole all the way through the board to simulate a marked board.

With the mockup complete, the offset washer provides lateral and linear adjustment of the bed boards and allows for various alignment options.

Mark the actual board from the bottom and through the cross-brace that will hold the bed to the frame for a custom effect.

The bed mounting bolts can be hidden under the wood planks, which requires some modification of the bottom of the boards to keep them flush to the braces. The carriage bolt on the cross-sill is where the eccentric or offset hole would have been in the board, mounting to the truck frame.

With the board marked from the bottom, use a round-head carbide burr and dome out the wood. Do this so that a carriage bolt doesn't push the board up when it's installed onto the truck frame and the floor remains perfectly flush.

This looks very clean, is much less time consuming to prep, and pays tribute to the vintage look and feel of the truck. If the bed needs to be adjusted for alignment to the cab, I may have to slot the frame mounts a little, but that's a minimal price to pay for a tidy looking bed floor.

corners to relieve pressure and move boards into place while the other person was in the bed with boards and adjustment tools. Regardless, it's a challenge that I accept, and I enjoy thinking my way through obstacles and performing tasks without creating damage. Using this vintage high-lift jack with a block of wood works well and doesn't damage the paint. The goal is to lift the corners of the bed one at a time to reinstall the 3/4-inch bed boards and realign the bed with the cab. With some careful planning, it's easily done.

It may seem redundant to label everything during reassembly, but it's a good practice. When reassembling custom or vintage restored cars, there's no such thing as being too careful in reassembly. If one of the boards was placed incorrectly, it would change the orientation of the grain pattern, and each board has a unique appearance and slight variation in the pattern and stain color. All of these details need to be considered. The use of labels helps you remember what you decided during mockup and is the best way to have an easy and high-quality installation when it comes to final assembly.

If you are aiming for an original restoration, use painted or powder coated steel strips and hardware, as well as the offset alignment bolts that hold the bed to the chassis from the top. However, I prefer the look of polished stainless strips and fasteners and the lack of the offset bolts

     TRUCK BEDS How to Install, Restore, and Modify

The new kit is laid out, and the grain is sorted to be the way it was planned. At this point, the boards have been numbered on the bottom side so that I don't lose track of placement. I used refinishing techniques shown in this book, including a Golden Oak stain, which was followed by multiple coats of polyurethane satin finish to get a beautiful and durable coating on the boards.

Starting from the sides and working inward, drill the marked pilot holes from the mockup out to 3/8-inch holes. This gives the bolts a little play, which is necessary for adjustments during assembly.

The numbers show the placement of the boards from left to right. This is an important step because all of the boards need to line up with the metal retaining strips that utilize predrilled holes in the cross-sills for mounting.

A few important tools include a soft-faced (dead-blow) hammer, drift pins of various sizes, and pry bars. I am using a fully refinished wood kit that took many hours to surface and stain. Adjustments need to be minimal to avoid scratches and damage.

Prying against the cross-sill will lift the wheel housing up enough to slide the outside boards in without contact to the metal bedside.

   TRUCK BEDS How to Install, Restore, and Modify

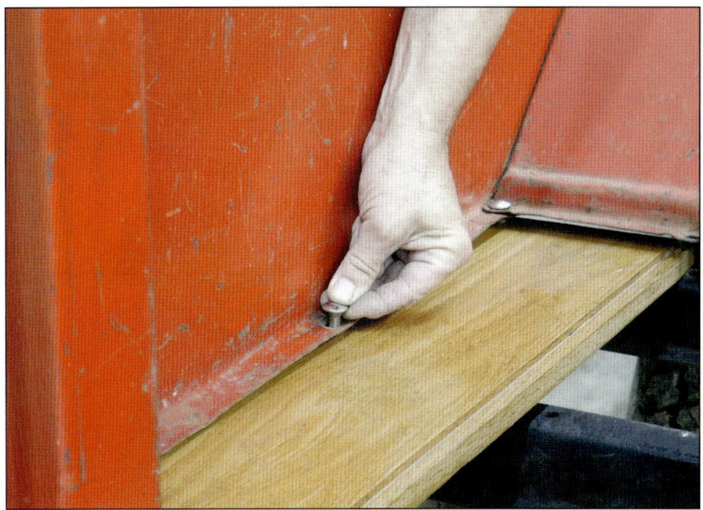

This view shows how you can use the drift tool and adjust one hole to align the others. Be careful during this process. Small adjustments are necessary. You may need to pin one bolt on one side to hold the board's position while adjusting the other end. Bolts are just dropped onto the holes and nuts aren't added until everything has a basic alignment established.

Carriage bolts are larger for the outside boards and are dropped in place. Make sure that they're seated properly in the square stamped holes.

The soft-faced hammer has enough heft to move the wood easily without damaging or bruising the edges of the boards.

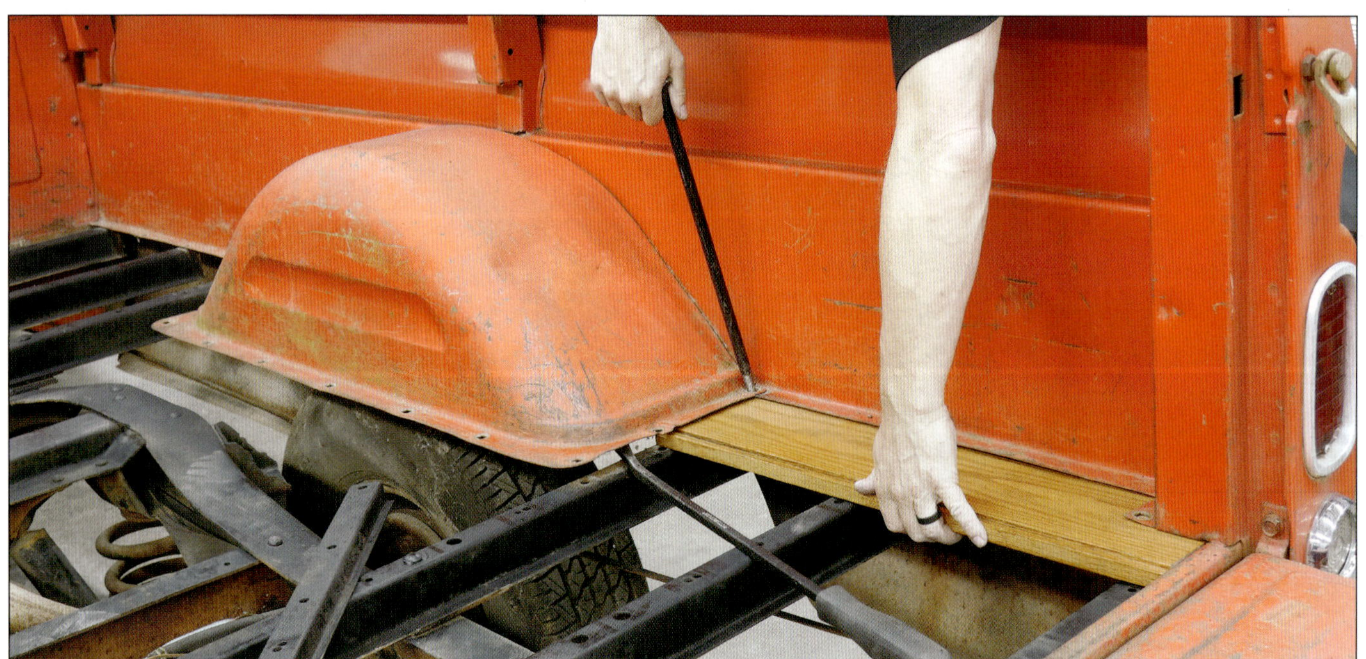

On the opposite side of the bed, a floor jack with a wood block can be used under the bedside to relieve pressure from the cross-sills. The boards that were fitted on the left side now have the bed unbalanced with uneven pressure.

The combination of a drift tool and pry bar on the right side boards is enough to drop down carriage bolts along the perimeter of the bedside. A second set of hands really help this process, but it can be done with one person.

    TRUCK BEDS How to Install, Restore, and Modify

mind knowing that the fuel tank is not only protected by the frame rails but it's also a far distance from the driver and passenger if an accident occurs. I plan on keeping this truck as a fun weekend driver, and there are several more safety upgrades that will happen before it goes back on the road again.

for a cleaner appearance. There is very little maintenance on polished stainless-steel strips, and they'll never rust.

I moved the fuel tank behind the rear axle for several reasons. These trucks originally had the tank behind the seat of the cab, but it's now a custom truck by definition due to the change. However, I won't miss the fuel smell every time I get into the cab, and it gives me peace of

The trend of patina being cool won't go away any time soon. Finding a skilled shop to restore bodywork and the cost of buying materials to do it yourself are factors that keep some people from committing to

You will get good at the process of using the drift and dropping bolts into the holes! Sixty-plus-year-old sheet metal has a way of finding unintended shapes and needs some work to go back into form.

Place a marked piece of masking tape along the rear edge of the bed floor. This acts as a reminder as to which boards go in what location. It also protects painted surfaces if you're working on a finished restoration.

During the mockup phase of this kit, the bottom of the boards was domed to accommodate the head of the carriage bolt that mounts the bed to the chassis. The carriage bolts were welded in earlier, and with them now under the wood, it provides a much cleaner look.

Using one of the bed strips, I can easily align the boards for installation of all the strips. This is a quick check of the spacing and helps to be able to drop the bolts into their homes quickly.

     TRUCK BEDS How to Install, Restore, and Modify

The wheel housing on the driver's side had enough of a gap to slide the end strip between the wood and steel without scratching or forcing anything. Then, the bolts hold it all in place.

Carriage bolts for the center strips are smaller than the perimeter bolts, but they serve the same purpose.

restoring the sheet metal on a truck. Personally, I think it's cool to have a brand-new bed floor right up against faded, chipped-out paint. I've also seen freshly painted steel wheels look great against a "survivor" paint job. The other truth is this: the original bed on the project truck was literally falling out as it drove down the road, and it was unsafe to place a payload in the bed. Installing a new bed restores the functional use of the truck.

I can have fun in this truck for many more years before I commit to a full restoration. How do you eat an elephant? One bite at a time. With about 40 hours of labor and a reasonable financial investment, the truck will be usable again. To me, that's a win, and it translates to about five or six bites out of this elephant.

If you're a one-man show like I am most times, you need to get creative. Nuts get installed on the bolts from the bottom, and the battery holds them firmly in place so that they can be easily tightened from the bottom. Make sure that you use a pad of sorts—and a clean battery. Other heavy objects may be a better choice depending on what is available.

　　TRUCK BEDS　How to Install, Restore, and Modify

Most of the hardware is easily to access, but a swivel socket may be needed in some instances. This kit comes with locknuts with a serrated washer on the backside so that there is no need for lock washers on the smaller carriage bolts.

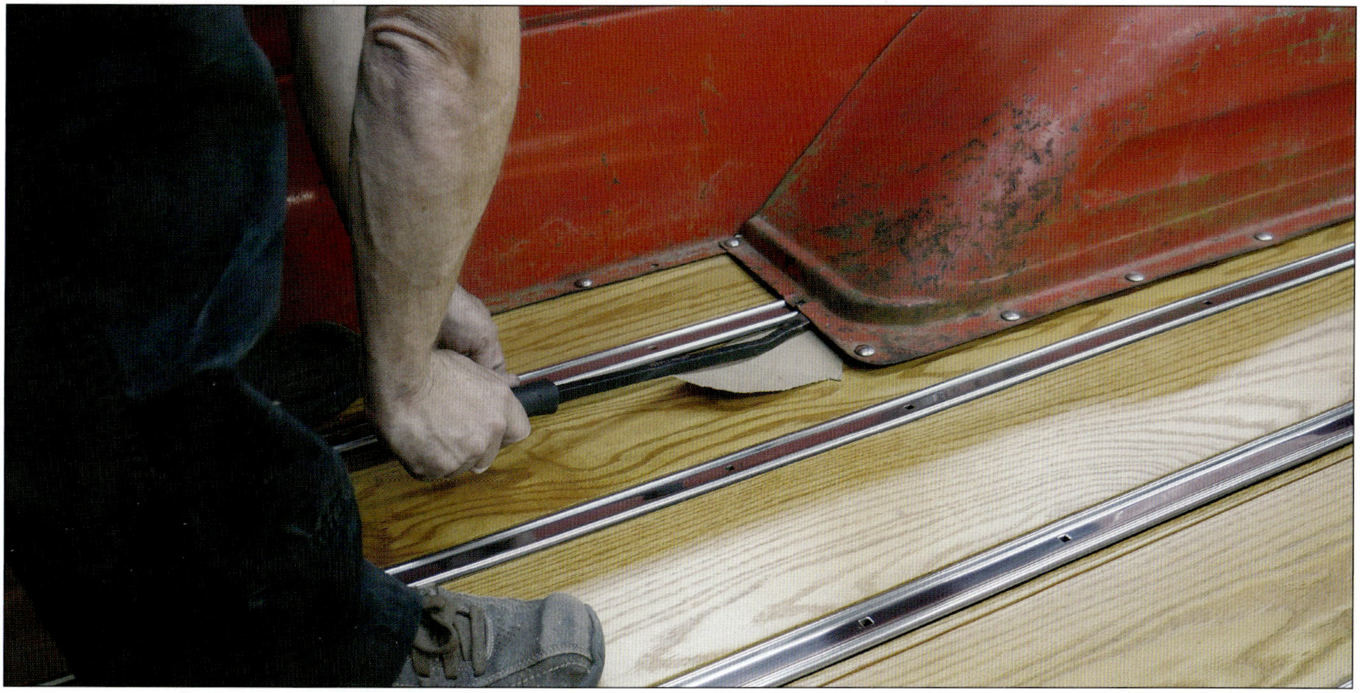

There was a tighter fit for the passenger's side front strip ahead of the wheel housing. A pry bar gets the metal off the wood so that the strip can be installed, and a piece of heavy cardboard protects the wood floor from damage.

Since this truck's fuel tank has been relocated from inside the cab to behind the axle for a variety of reasons, I will drill for a fuel door in one of the boards (board number-7 in our case). I'm measuring to find the center of the fuel tank opening.

With board number-7 back in place, I transposed my measurements onto the board, which is protected with masking tape so that I don't damage the finish.

With the centerline established and the location double-checked, start with a pilot hole for the hole saw.

A 1-1/2-inch hole saw on a low speed drills through the oak plank slowly but without drama or tearing the edges.

Carefully sand around the opening to remove any rough wood from the saw and create a slight chamfer on the edge for easy installation of the fuel door.

Reseal the wood to protect it from moisture or fuel penetration. Moisture can leech under the finished surface and cause delamination over time. Sealing it now prevents that from happening.

This truck's fuel door is domed stainless steel, and it will look great against the polished strips in the floor. Use a speed square to align the screw holes.

A 1/8-inch pilot hole allows the slightly larger screws to seat properly without splitting the wood. Pilot holes should be made before drilling a hole in any woodworking project.

Align the board to the filler neck of the tank. I spent a lot of time to make sure that it would all fit properly.

A rubber gasket seals the top of the filler door and helps protect the wood surface from bruising.

Use the alignment tool to keep the screw holes in the proper orientation. The rubber filler neck was clamped from the bottom side with radiator-hose clamps.

TRUCK BEDS How to Install, Restore, and Modify

Now, install the final two bed strips and bolt down on both sides of board number-7. Make a final inspection before tightening the hardware from the bottom.

In the passenger's side rear corner, you can see that the bed-strip bolts that are between planks use a large fender washer (usually included in the kit) and smaller flat washers followed by a lock washer on the larger perimeter bolts. Flat washers provide more clamping force and help with alignment on the top side.

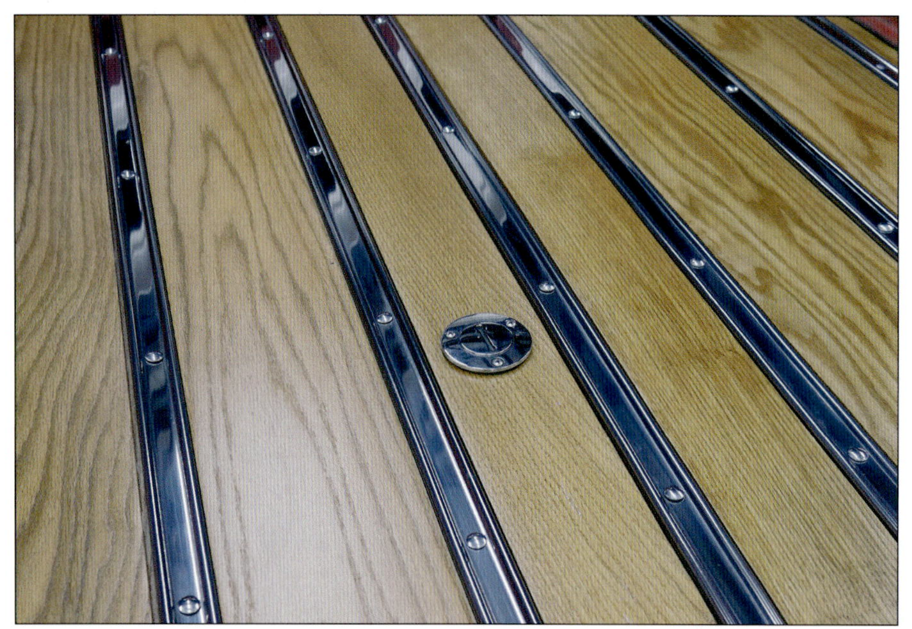

Do a final inspection to check for even spacing on the boards before tightening everything. Remember that wood is not perfect, and your truck may be many decades old. If you don't get a perfect fit, remember that these vehicles were far from perfect when they rolled off the assembly line.

After some minor adjustments and at least an hour of snugging down bolts while riding a creeper, you will have a beautiful result. Here, the satin finish of the oak wood against polished stainless steel is stunning.

TRUCK BEDS How to Install, Restore, and Modify

Making Your Own Bed Boards

If you're ambitious, handy, inspired, or all three, making a bed floor can be a very rewarding project. This book shows how to create a single board with simple hand tools, although you may need to borrow or invest in some tools to complete the job.

A must-have item is a router with several different bits, and an edge guide needs to be used if you don't have a fixture or table. The home center or lumberyard can provide a number of options for wood variety, and the internet is full of exotic wood suppliers if you want to try something out of the box. Selecting each board carefully is important. Most lumber piles are picked

A dust mask, leather gloves, and eye and ear protection are vital. If you create a lot of dust, use an extraction device (or at least a good exhaust fan).

As with any tool that has a sharp blade that spins fast, proper personal protective equipment (PPE) is important! Eye protection, respiratory protection, and skin protection is the bare minimum.

If possible, do woodworking in a well-ventilated and well-lit area. Practice on a scrap board until you figure out how to control the router and to achieve the distance and thickness of the notches and grooves.

You can decide to make your own boards, and the old boards can be used as a template. Dust off your woodworking tools and either buy pre-milled boards or (depending on your tools on hand) start with rough-cut lumber and completely make your own floor kit. This is a stack of curly maple that is ready for the milling process at Bed-Wood in Kentucky.

I went to the local home center and bought a 1x8 pine plank, which is actually 3/4 x 7 inches. Inspect your boards carefully and be aware of knots, cracks, or sap, all of which can affect the finish.

These boards are relatively inexpensive but have damage, including these chips in the corner, which have to be trimmed. Consider buying oversized lengths and trimming to your size.

TRUCK BEDS How to Install, Restore, and Modify

These gouges can sometimes be repaired by using moisture and a soldering iron to re-expand the grain of the wood. I'll just trim this piece off and use the undamaged face.

Knots add character and look great in the planks. However, there can be porosity or divots around the knots. Just be aware that you may have to use filler if you don't want to have small flaws in your boards.

over by craftsmen who know what to look for. Reject the lumber with cracks, ugly knots, and splits.

The image on the bottom right is a precut board from another kit and shows the design that fits the stainless-steel bed strips. The rabbet (notch) is cut into each side of the board, which is followed by a 1/4-inch groove to hold the strip edges in place. Doing this freehand is likely impossible, so use a universal edge guide for consistency. The guide is adjustable and makes it easy to create the edges on the board.

Pay particular attention to the end of the boards as you draw near. When you're handheld with a router, it's easy for the tool to get loose at the end of the board and for your lines to waiver. The centrifugal force of the spinning blade will try to direct the tool as well, so steady, slow, and consistent delivery is the key to a consistent groove.

Trees are round, and the grain always has an arc to it. When you establish the face side (top side) of the boards, have the arc toward the middle of the board. As the wood expands, it cups and forms a depression that holds water. Avoid cupping by making sure that the end-grain shows a dome toward the top side in the pattern rather than a cup.

I used this router with a 3/4-inch straight-sided bit and a 1/4-inch bit to cut the groove on the inside edge. Freehand cuts are risky and inconsistent, so use an edge guide as well.

Use some scrap boards to practice and set your bit height and distance off the edge.

I used a soft-faced sanding block and 180-grit sandpaper to clean up the sharp edges and slivers on the end-grain. Don't round over the edges too much, but eliminate the sharp corners to give the board a professional appearance. Be aware that most dual-action sanders are a long stroke (5/16 inch) and are designed to remove as much material as possible. A finish sander has a much smaller 3/32-inch stroke and won't introduce visible circular sanding marks on the surface. If you're hand sanding, always sand in the direction of the grain (not across the grain). Most likely, cross-grain sanding will show through the finish topcoats. When using a short-stroke dual-action sander, such as the 3/32-inch Surf-Prep electric sander, it doesn't matter as long as you keep the tool flat against the wood surface.

Expect to invest a couple of hours sanding each board. This translates to a few days of work to complete this project once you understand the tools and procedures. Even if you have to invest a few hundred dollars into tools (a router, edge guide, and bits), you're still way ahead financially of buying a completed kit, which can run upward of $1,000 and much more if you opt for an exotic wood. I enjoy learning, and the thought of making my own floor is much less intimidating now that I've written it out for this book. If you invest in yourself, you'll reap the reward.

1 *It takes some time to get the feel for this. Notice the weird jog in the edge where I wasn't pressing the edge guard enough as well as the place where I leaned outward on the router and it gouged the rabbet. These issues are why practice is important.*

2 *With the bed board clamped to the table, begin on one end and move slowly but deliberately, putting pressure against the side of the board as well as downward pressure on the shoe of the router.*

3 *The bit is spinning more than 20,000 rpm, so this equipment demands respect. It takes me a careful 30-40 seconds for each side of an 8-foot board.*

4 *With the first 3/4-inch cut completed on both sides, change bits and get ready for the 1/4-inch groove. Whenever changing bits on your router, take the extra step of unplugging it from the outlet or extension cord. Accidentally turning on the router while changing bits can cause serious injuries.*

5 *These bits cost about $20 each, but they rarely go dull unless you hit nails or nick the corners. The 3/4-inch bit on the left became discolored while being used on hardwood, but the blade is still very sharp.*

6 *Practicing again on the scrap piece, set the groove for the proper depth, which is 1/8 inch down from the 3/4-inch rabbet cut.*

7 *This is exactly what I wanted. Now, I can run both sides of the pine board.*

8 *Use the same careful pace with both cuts. It's easy to lose focus and damage the board, so concentration is important.*

9 *My grandfather taught me basic woodshop skills, and regular cleanup was one of them. A broom and dustpan instead of an air hose keeps the air more breathable and makes less of a mess on the benches and toolbox.*

10 *Using 220-grit sandpaper on a soft block, sanding the sharp corners on the newly cut lumber.*

11 *To sand the face of the boards, I used an electric dual-action sander with a 3/32-inch stroke, which was hooked up to my wet/dry vacuum cleaner to keep the dust down. The short stroke of the sander makes a very smooth cut and doesn't interfere with the grain and how it looks through the stain.*

12 *These lines against the grain of the wood are from the thickness planer at the mill. The sander levels them out so that they don't show through the finish.*

13 *A technique that I picked up at BedWood is to chamfer the bottom ends of the boards so that there is no interference as the boards sit in the stamped-steel bed parts. This can be done by hand and only requires a sanding block and 180-grit sandpaper.*

14 *The finished board allows the steel strips to be countersunk but still slightly higher than the surface. This protects the wood under load, and the 1/4-inch groove provides enough wood expansion room. Now, I'm ready for the topcoats.*

    TRUCK BEDS How to Install, Restore, and Modify

CHAPTER 3

Custom Wood Floor Options

This bed has an interesting mix of custom features. There are high-gloss body-worked and painted areas, a texturized coating under the metallic topcoat over the extended wheel tubs, a finely finished exotic wood floor system that ties into sheet-metal extensions fore and aft of the wheel, and polished bed strips that act as accent pieces of trim rather than functional fasteners over the boards. The bed strips on this custom truck are very important in the overall design of its floor, and careful attention to detail is required. The bed strips serve the traditional function of holding the boards in place, and they also provide detail for the entire build and can carry the theme of the vehicle. The polished, boltless strips on this stunning 1963 F-100 built by Painthouse are polished to a mirror finish and bring the color of the paint into the reflection. (Photo Courtesy Randy Borcherding)

Personalizing trucks has been a tradition since the beginning of hot rodding. The bed floor is a perfect canvas to individualize a truck and make it unique, and there are countless ways to customize a traditional wood floor in a vintage pickup.

In this chapter, I'll illustrate several custom wood floor finishing options, such as waterborne, urethane, and custom painted options.

BedWood is an award-winning, high-quality bed floor manufacturer in Hopkinsville, Kentucky, that specializes in custom and original replacement bed floors for vintage and modern trucks. The company also manufactures stainless-steel bed-strip kits and replacement parts for several other manufacturers, having developed proprietary equipment to manufacture bed floor retaining strips.

Metal strips were created to hold down the bed boards in a truck and to keep the wood from shifting under a load. They also made it

This stack of polished stainless-steel bed strips is ready for shipment. BedWood makes traditional exposed bolt strips as well as several different hidden-bolt styles. These kits come complete with all of the hardware for mounting and installation, all of which is packaged in-house and sent to the customer.

The stainless-steel strips begin with flat stock on a coil. This heavy-gauge, polished stainless steel is sourced from American manufacturers and carefully selected. It is fed from a coil into the proprietary equipment that was created for this process.

TRUCK BEDS How to Install, Restore, and Modify

From the coil, the stainless steel is fed into a pressing die machine that feeds the flat stock into a series of presses, punches, and jaws that form the steel. Stainless steel is an extremely hard and dense metal. This provides the capability of great strength with minimal wall thickness once it is stamped and manipulated into a shape. Consider the stainless-steel hubcaps from the cars of the 1950s and 1960s. They were stamped from very thin-walled stainless steel into decorative and functional wheel covers. Those wheel covers were able to withstand incredible amounts of weight and pressure without damage because of the tension held in the metal after pressing. Once polished, stainless steel retains its gloss almost permanently and seldom succumbs to oxidation.

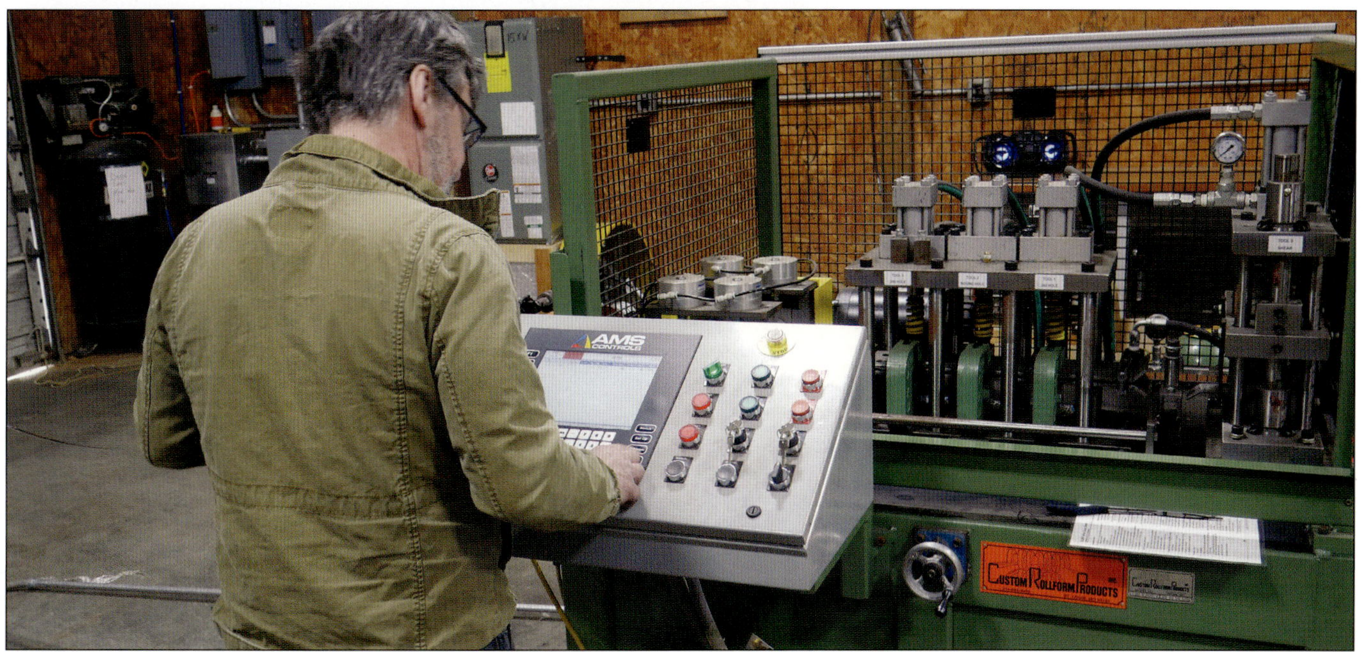

An operator programs the machine by setting up the type of holes and lengths that are needed. This is determined by the batch of strips the shop will press at that time. Typically, there's at least a six-month backup in stock, and inventory is constantly upgraded.

Quality control is critical at every stage of manufacturing. After careful inspection of a test piece, the machine is programmed for a full run of strips. The operator looks for symmetry in the edges as well as consistency of the punched square holes that hold the carriage bolts in place.

After pressing, the strips are inspected again and spot-polished (if necessary) before being carefully put into organized inventory. They are then packaged for orders and shipped to customers.

TRUCK BEDS How to Install, Restore, and Modify

Bed strips are excellent accent pieces to the natural wood surface and provide a natural visual break. Just as chrome and stainless-steel trim can accent the exterior panels of a vehicle, bed strips are an important component to the overall design of a bed floor. Functional clamping strips are available from BedWood if you want to put your truck to work. I've used this style of clamping retainers in car haulers, and they're incredibly strong while still being low profile and not interfering with the floor clearance on low vehicles.

Hardware needs to be consistently high quality and complete for each kit. BedWood has staff on hand that packs its own hardware based on the order. BedWood employees polish stainless-steel fasteners onsite to match polished strips or will ship "natural" stainless. Each order is carefully inspected before shipping for quality control. If someone requests non-polished hardware that's to be painted to match the

possible to replace a single wooden board in a bed floor if it is damaged, which saves the process of replacing the whole floor. Bed strips provide many options to the overall appearance of the floor and provide many ways to customize a bed. Boltless strips are a great option. They provide a clean look while retaining the original floor construction and the vintage style of the linear strips with a nod toward the custom look. Billet aluminum strips are another option. They give a unique and clean look. Aluminum strips can be ordered with several different manufacturers of wood kits, with BedWood being one.

original paint, raw stainless kits can be shipped. The advantage to this over the factory carbon-steel hardware is that it will never rust—even if the paint gets chipped off. This gives it a much longer life than the original nuts, bolts, and strips, and it ensures that the new components will probably outlast the owner of the truck.

Craftsmanship Meets Computer-Controlled Automation

The saying goes: "quality in, quality out." Each raw board is carefully inspected multiple times for damage, character, and integrity. Wood is an imperfect substrate, and it's guaranteed to have flaws, but just like fine leather, how it was raised, where it grew, what conditions it was exposed to during its life, and especially how it was harvested make a huge difference in the quality and appearance. The boards are inspected many times at BedWood to not only ensure a great outcome but also to maximize the character of the wood and have continuity within the set of boards in a kit.

If you've ever taken woodworking classes, you'll be instantly reminded of it when walking into the BedWood factory. The odor of wood chips, sawdust, and machine oil all have a distinctive odor.

Workers at this plant are selected for their skill and background, and they are trained internally to become accustomed to the high-quality demands to produce a premium product. My grandfather was a carpenter by trade and always had a workshop set up in his garage. Just like the interior of an antique car, milled woods each have a distinctive scent, so the tour was like going back in time for me.

Bed systems are a mix of automation and skilled hand labor. Computer-controlled machinery is very precise and consistent, but

Rough-cut lumber sits on these pallets at BedWood headquarters. Each board is carefully inspected before shipment from the source, again upon delivery, and again as it's stacked. Only the finest lumber makes its way to the manufacturing facility. Wood with flaws or damage is not used. Some repairs can be made to subtle splits in some boards, but if done incorrectly, the glue can show through a finish coat and affect the look of the floor.

The process of manufacturing a truck bed wood kit begins with the hand-selected rough-cut wood that is fed through a thickness planer. A small layer of wood is removed from each side of the boards to provide a smooth and consistent flat surface. These 12-foot boards are ready to go.

TRUCK BEDS How to Install, Restore, and Modify

The planer mils both sides of each board to a pre-specified thickness, depending on the kit that's being processed. Very little waste wood is generated, as the lengths are carefully chosen for maximum usage.

Chips are extracted and later resold to local vendors that use wood as a consumable. Local barbecue restaurants love this place. They can get many woods of different varieties that add to the character of the local cuisine. The end of this first step shows the beautiful exposed grain of this board.

After being sent through the thickness planer, these oak boards are trimmed to a rough width. Although the machines are programmed, the technician has complete control of the process. The boards are not hand-hewn, but they're carefully overseen and nurtured through these processes.

Once the boards are cut to width, they are fed into another machine that finishes the edges with a rabbet cut and a groove on both sides at once. This can be done with hand tools, but the semiautomated process provides incredible precision and fast turnaround on these boards to maximize efficiency.

     TRUCK BEDS How to Install, Restore, and Modify

The finished, trimmed boards are ready for the next step. Even though machinery is involved, each step is carefully overseen by craftsmen who have decades of experience. In these initial milling steps, the boards are repeatedly inspected for flaws or damage before going further into the process.

After each board is cut to length, the end-grain is beveled to keep any cracks or splits from developing. This also provides a better fit to the stamped-steel bed ends that are stamped in mass-production environments and are inconsistent. They may not have a perfect 90-degree bend that the wood needs to sit into. The bevel on the end-grain goes on every board and serves two purposes: to improve fitment and longevity.

After the edges are refined and the boards are designated with their placement within the kit, select side boards are clamped to a CNC routing table to be trimmed at preprogrammed shapes to fit the various bed designs. Each wheel-housing on each bed floor has a distinct shape, so these pieces must be carefully inventoried for proper packaging and accuracy.

nothing replaces the judgement and individual attention to each part that a trained and skilled technician can deliver. Automation speeds up processes so that people can lend human touch and craftsmanship. Although some BedWood employees were relegated to their work stations, most were cross-trained to fill several positions, depending on the workload of the day. Bedwood's in-house designers play a very important role in maintaining quality control of the products and oversee the design concept-to-manufacturing transitions at every step.

Sanding is one of the last steps in the process. It is done with a belt-fed system that feeds and sands the boards through several different grits, finishing with 220-grit sandpaper. It is then ready for stain and topcoats. Various sanding belts are hanging on the wall. The wood type determines which grit is used. This is a mix of industrial machining with fine-finish woodworking techniques.

After the sanding process and another detailed inspection, the boards are organized into sets and are staged for either raw wood delivery (for the end user to stain and finish) or to be sent to the finish-application booth. This set is receiving a natural wood finish with just a high-quality polyurethane. Both sides and the ends receive several coats and are allowed to air dry.

Finish Coatings and Options

For refinishing and refinish training, it doesn't matter what the substrate is, the process is fascinating. Waterborne products have been permanently added into automotive refinishing, and there's a surprisingly similar crossover between woodworking and metal restoration and repair.

With wood, water-based products are absorbed into the pores of the wood. Wood also requires mechanical adhesion by profiling, which means that the surface needs to be sanded.

On metal, most times a porous coating, such as epoxy primer, is required to give the porosity and chemical bond to the harder metal surfaces. Although epoxy is an excellent coating for wood substrates and allows

This set of boards will be packaged as a complete kit once they are fully cured. Each board is labeled and given an identification number for each specific kit. Dozens of kits leave BedWood over the course of a month, destined for customers all over the world.

TRUCK BEDS How to Install, Restore, and Modify

This is a proprietary waterborne finish called "carbon." It is incredibly strong. Being water based, it bonds to the pores of the wood and acts as a sealer, color, and topcoat all in one. The carbon finish is very attractive, as it shows the grain of the wood in shadows and highlights but has a deep black luster under certain lights.

This is an example of the carbon finish on a RetroLiner system in a late-model GM truck. The grain is easily seen, and the semisolid finish still has depth to the outward appearance.

The BedWood showroom has a sample of all the finishes that are available, with samples of various finishes on various types of wood. There's no limit to how creative you can get with these kits.

the use of all automotive coatings to be applied to wood, it covers the grain and takes away from the wood's natural beauty. Water-based stains and polyurethanes allow the wood grain to show through, which is the reason that those coatings are so prevalent in woodworking, furniture, and instrument making.

Immortalizing a Memory

A now-custom 1966 Chevrolet C10 pickup was passed down many years ago from James Otto's grandfather Pete. A vehicle can become a symbol of memories, which is certainly the case with James' pro-touring-styled C-10 named *Pete's Sake*. It's a stunning custom

If you order a kit "natural," you can take on the top-coating duties yourself and purchase the finishing products straight from the manufacturer. Whether you order yours ready to install or decide to have a hand in the process, there's virtually no finish that can't be achieved.

Country music star James Otto chose a BedWood custom floor for his C-10 project Pete's Sake, which was named after his grandfather Pete. It's a pro touring–style build that features a custom pearl paint job and many body modifications by custom builder Brent Buttrey as well as Triworks Hot Rods in Nashville.

pickup that was built in tribute to his late grandfather and is in the spirit of the man as well.

Styling and custom work is aggressive and subtle at the same time. The more you look, the more you can identify the modifications that were painstakingly created by the crew at Triworks Hot Rods and by Brent Buttrey, who are friends of James and reputable car builders in the Nashville, Tennessee, area.

There's almost no limit to the style, color, and surface quality that can be created on wood. As coatings evolve, so do the options for a high-quality and durable wood finish for truck beds as well as ways to make custom designs. If you have limited time or skills to complete a

The ultra-clean design of the truck is impressive. The wood floor features painted boltless strips and a satin finish on maple wood. Notice the extra wide wheel tubs that indicate a large tire footprint.

bed-floor project and need someone to send a turnkey, ready-to-install floor system for your truck (antique or late model), it's helpful to know that options exist where your imagination is the only limitation.

Etched into the bed floor is a memorable photo of James and his grandfather Pete. It serves as a reminder to James of how important family is and of his love for Pete. This is an amazing personal memorial with a unique and very creative way to memorialize a warm memory and a prized possession.

CHAPTER 4

ALUMINUM BED FLOORS

Whether you have a wild custom like this 1971 C-10 called C-Tane or a traditional restoration, it's great to have options for the most visible part of the truck. An alternative to custom wood floors is gaining popularity in the custom and original bed floor replacement market: aluminum bed boards that are wrapped in a highly durable vinyl coating. These boards can show high-resolution images of everything from a traditional wood grain to any style of graphic that can be produced with a computer and good designer, such as those at Smokey Road Rod Shop (www.smokeyroadroadshop.com) in Georgia. The extruded aluminum boards, ease of installation, multiple bed-strip options, and unlimited finish options make this a very interesting choice.

When you design a truck that's as aggressively styled as *C-Tane*, which was built on Season 3 of my *Hands-On Cars* television series, the last thing you want to do is disappoint people as they look into the bed area and see a typical wood system. This truck, due to the Schwartz G-Machine chassis, had to have the bed floor raised 3 inches to allow for suspension travel, so the opportunity to do something cool and custom presented itself very early in the build. Frankly, it was a problem to be solved, but much the same as most hot rodding projects, it turned into the focal point of the entire truck.

It can be debated whether the aluminum extrusions should be called boards, but given the location and

context in which the product was designed to replace actual boards, the name fits. So, they'll be referred to as boards in this book.

One of the benefits to this system is minimal expansion and contraction of the aluminum boards, which makes them extremely stable during temperature cycles and virtually eliminates the possibility of boards cracking or shrinking over time. There are many different digitized grains available to be laminated onto the boards, and the grains are taken from scanned sequential boards in a stack of actual milled lumber. So, even the printed wood grain features incredible realism.

The dividing strips are either aluminum or stainless steel and utilize a groove in the underside that allows mounting hardware to be slid into and aligned with the cross-sills. This provides great versatility in mounting options whether you're installing into a vintage truck or into a custom project like *C-Tane*.

Raising the bed floor is common in many custom street trucks these days, whether the need comes from an aggressive suspension drop or performance chassis modifications that require more suspension travel. A custom C-notch may require a complete floor modification in the

The back side of the extruded "boards" shows where they get their strength, utilizing the center brace as well as the side structure. You can see the vinyl wrap around the ends, and the identification labels for each color. Another benefit of this floor system is that it's at least 100 pounds lighter than a conventional wood floor.

Stainless-steel hardware that attaches to the board's dividing strips holds the system together. These fasteners are anti-corrosive by nature and last much longer than carbon steel bolts that eventually rust, even when coated with paint.

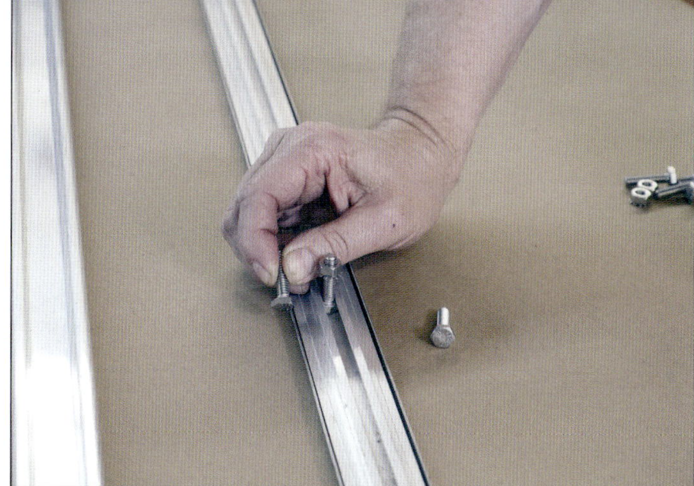

This is an example of the way the fasteners slide into the groove of a bed strip. They're easily moveable to adjust into the cross-sills and feature a locknut to secure them.

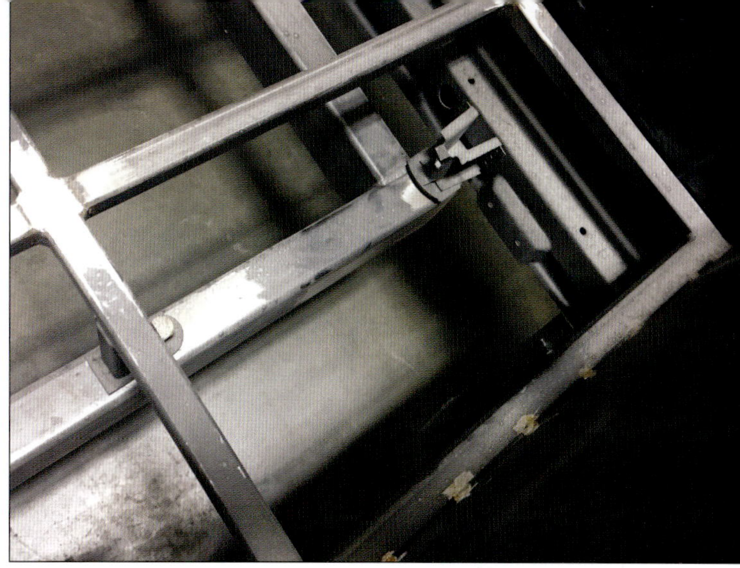

This is a custom application that needs the bed floor raised to clear suspension parts. The factory cross-sills are used to mount the bed to the chassis, and a secondary floor support was fabricated to support the raised bed floor.

form of a tunnel or just moving the entire floor up past the chassis to accommodate the suspension. *C-Tane* needed a modest 3 inches but also had the addition of extra-wide wheel tubs to work around. So, a structural frame was constructed from 1-inch square tubing that was welded to the typically removable bedsides and front and rear panels.

This creates an assembly that with the flooring removed still provides access for chassis, suspension, or fuel-delivery maintenance. The finished appearance is stunning and fulfills the requirements of a visual focal point. The project name and logo were designed by Steve Longacre, digitized by Smokey Road Rod Shop, and applied to the aluminum boards. The floor system was framed with brushed-aluminum strips, and the boards around the tubs were left unframed for a unique floating appearance.

C-Tane uses extra-wide wheel tubs to accommodate an extremely wide wheel and tire combination. The 1-inch square tubing was used to create a level and very strong foundation for the new custom floor. Detailed measurements were sent to Smokey Road along with photos, vector artwork of the floor design, and a layout diagram. After a phone call to discuss details, the floor was built offsite and shipped for assembly after the truck was painted.

The finished floor is stunning and is a centerpiece for a cool custom truck. The carbon-fiber pattern on the boards along with the project name provide a custom touch, and the boltless bed strips are a throwback to traditional bed floor design, which fits this vintage C-10 perfectly. A fuel door sits above the tank and is easily reachable with the gate open. The end boards are capped with brushed-aluminum angle stock and serve as an attractive transition from the boards to the gate.

This 1966 C-10 has a much more traditional floor, which still utilizes a Smokey Road bed system. These beds are American made, maintenance-free, and more scuff and scratch resistant than a traditional finished wood floor.

TRUCK BEDS How to Install, Restore, and Modify

Aluminum Bed Floor in a Traditional Restoration Project

Aluminum bed floors for vintage vehicles are a recent and excellent creative choice for replacing a traditional or original bed floor. One option features an extruded aluminum board system as well as a unique design of boltless or exposed fastener strips.

American ingenuity was the driver for this new bed system, due to the Smokey Road Rod Shop in south Georgia wanting to provide more options than were available with wood with benefits that wood simply could not offer.

Wood floors can be refinished in many ways and styled with a lot of character by using traditional wood finishes, exotic grains, and creativity. Utilizing the ability to print digital images or artwork that has a very strong ultraviolet (UV) resistance and physical surface strength is a bonus. Creating a bed-floor system that combines those aesthetic benefits to a system weighing more than 100 pounds less than a traditional wood-floor system opens a whole new set of possibilities. Since these

The identification label of the finish is shown. This isn't a computer graphic of an imagined wood grain, this is an actual digitized image of "true Growth" wood to keep a faithful and authentic appearance to the floor system.

Installation will take you about 3 to 4 hours, but that depends on the condition of your existing cross-sills. Simple hand tools and a drill are the only tools required.

You can see where the factory cross-sills have been redrilled to fit the hidden bolts instead of the carriage bolts of a traditional bed floor. With the strip upside down, you can mark the location of the bolt in the slide channel and align all of the fasteners before flipping the strips around and dropping them into place.

With the strips dropped in place, slide the groove in the side of the board under the edge of the strip and loosely drop it in position. This is similar to laminate flooring.

With several boards and strips in place, reach under and get the 7/16-inch-head locknuts hand threaded loosely onto the accessible studs. This keeps things stable as the bed floor is assembled and saves a little time under the truck later.

systems come premeasured and designed to fit into an existing bed assembly and truck chassis, typical installation should only take about 3 or 4 hours with simple hand tools.

You'll probably have to drill the boards around the perimeter of the bed, and drilling cross-sills is required to accommodate mounting hardware. If you understand how to use a tape measure and a ruler, you'll have no problems installing one of these systems.

With pro-touring and race trucks gaining massive popularity, weight always factors into the performance of a vehicle. Weight over the rear axle is never a bad thing, especially on a typically nose-heavy pickup, but eliminating 100 pounds can make a serious difference in a competition. Also, being able to control the weight of your truck and not be a victim of tradition provides a new freedom when building your dream truck.

With today's modern suspension systems, C-notches, air springs, and even cantilever suspensions, many custom trucks have a raised bed floor. These aluminum bed floors provide a way to easily raise the floor to accommodate chassis modifications as well as create easy access in case the floor needs to be disassembled for maintenance or repair. The interesting ability to use digital graphics allows another level or creativity—whether that means choosing the type of wood, color

TRUCK BEDS How to Install, Restore, and Modify

of the stain, or even deviating completely from a natural appearance.

Not everyone has woodworking skills, and even if you do, not everyone has the time or space it demands to do a proper refinishing job on a bed floor. Saving time is always big with me, and when I find a way to save time and still have stellar appearance it's always a win. These vinyl finishes are waterproof, stainproof, and UV resistant.

Wood, by its very nature, is porous and absorbs moisture, which creates expansion and contraction in weather and temperature cycles. At some point, when a wood bed floor is consistently exposed to the elements, its finish will separate from the wood, which is commonly referred to as delamination. It can be argued that aluminum on a microscopic level is porous, but not to the extent that it will expand and contract and pop off the finish. An aluminum floor may not be your cup of tea, and you may even insist on the traditional wood floor for history's sake, but you can't deny that this is an interesting alternative.

At a glance, you'd probably walk right past this truck at a cars-and-coffee event and never give the bed floor a second thought, other than maybe noticing the custom touch of the boltless polished stainless strips that hold the boards down. The tone of the wood is really worn, the grain looks authentic, and installation took only a few hours.

Keep all the fasteners loose until all of the boards and strips are in place because minor adjustments will be needed before tightening all the nuts from the bottom.

As light as the boards are, (20-percent lighter than a traditional wood system) the extrusions are very strong 6063-T6 aircraft-quality aluminum, which provides an extremely stable platform.

This total installation took about four hours, but it only had to happen once. With a traditional wood floor, I would've had to fully install the floor, drill, mock it up, and fit. Then, I'd have to disassemble the floor for refinishing, which would have taken about 20 hours for sanding, staining, sealing, polyurethane, and allowing for drying times. The new aluminum floor costs slightly more than a new wood kit, but it saves weight, time, and looks amazing. There's something to be said for getting your truck back on the road faster, and these modern alternatives provide more options than ever to personalize your truck.

When you consider the time that it takes to properly refinish an entire actual wood kit (between 20 and 40 hours), these systems start to check boxes and make a lot of sense. I love the innovation of manufactures such as Smokey Road Rod Shop and BedWood, and ultimately, us as end users, the technicians, car builders and consumers are the ones who really win out. The automotive aftermarket is full of cool designers with amazing products, and there's no sign of it stopping any time soon.

   TRUCK BEDS How to Install, Restore, and Modify

CHAPTER 5

Wood Floors for Modern Trucks

BedWood debuted the Retroliner in 2011 and has won several design awards for this innovative flooring system, including the Global Media award that was presented at SEMA in 2014. Retroliner is a modular wood flooring system that fits over the top of any modern truck's metal floor without the use of a destructive mounting system. Since this is the most noticeable panel on any truck, a wood floor serves a dual purpose: it ties the design back into the nostalgia of vintage trucks and protects the factory-painted floor. This floor is a proprietary finish that's exclusive to BedWood, and it is called the carbon series. It's an extremely strong finish coating, and with its beautiful ebony color, it contrasts with the bright red beautifully in this mid 1980s Chevrolet. Even better than how this system looks at home in a late-model truck is the fact that it's easy to install. It is also nondestructive because it doesn't even damage the paint on the metal floor of the host vehicle. (Photo Courtesy Jeff Major/BedWood)

Wood floors disappeared from modern passenger vehicles in 1987, last appearing in step-side trucks for Ford and General Motors. They last appeared on Dodge trucks in 1985.

I was a working collision-repair technician while these trucks were still considered to be current and relatively new, but there was no nostalgia surrounding the transition from wood floors to metal. The only things I was concerned about in the repair industry were the ability to do a fast and effective repair and get a good color match, which are also the objectives for those who perform collision repair today.

The process begins with a late-model truck bed being digitally scanned and plotted into a computer. BedWood uses state-of-the-art handheld scanners and compatible software for initial design work. It's important to have a perfect fit to the bottom profile of these modern truck bed floors, none of which are square anymore. Complex shapes are on every transition and panel in modern truck beds, and each has its own unique design. This technology allows BedWood to revise the designs quickly, keep up with production, and have very little downtime. There are many different liners with more than 40 wood-finish options that have been created for any truck with a metal floor up to 2022, including Jeeps, vans, El Caminos, and Rancheros. (Photo Courtesy Jeff Major/BedWood)

I have a 1966 Chevrolet C-10 that belonged to my father-in-law, Jack, since it was new, and both he and I used it as a daily driver work vehicle for many years. I remember hauling a load of pea gravel in it and looking back through the side mirror to see a dusty trail of gravel being evenly deposited onto the highway on the way back to the house—much to the aggravation of the traffic behind me. I cursed out the rotten wood planks for weeks afterward as I found ways to patch the holes and retain the use of that old truck before it needed a complete restoration.

In hindsight, the original bed floor lasted for more than 50 years under regular and heavy use. Many loads of firewood, gravel, pine straw, children's belongings, dance-recital equipment, bags of fertilizer, lawn mowers, and countless other overweight loads of miscellaneous stuff had been transported in the back of Jack's truck over those years.

Chapter 2 in this book shows the current state of my 1966 C-10, and although there have been changes to the engine and fuel system and there are plans for interior upgrades and air conditioning, this truck will still have some form of wood boards in the back. It just seems right to look over the bed rails and see wood planks at the bottom.

Today, I drive a late-model Dodge Ram with all the bells and whistles, and it's as comfortable to drive as any Cadillac I've ever driven. Trucks have truly evolved from "tractors with doors" to what is available today, but there's a fun nostalgia when driving a nearly 60-year-old truck. I also find myself disengaged by the super-shiny painted metal bed and want to do a faux floor made from wood, just to bring a little nostalgic character to the luxury truck.

Wood floors are a neat reminder that trucks evolved from primitive horse-drawn farming equipment into what is seen on today's roads in all their heavily optioned glory. It's arguable that mixed materials were not the best construction that could have been implemented to make a truck functional and strong, and everyone can concede that the bed floors of today's modern trucks are both easier to produce on assembly lines and easy to repair in a shop environment.

However, a wood floor is just plain cool and ties back to the iconic and practical detail. So, it's not a surprise that several companies are figuring out how to put a wood floor into a modern metal-floored pickup. You can now create a cool custom effect in a late-model truck by using a faux-floor that is inserted over the top of the manufacturer's steel flooring. This creates a neat vintage appearance (a retro style, if you will) and even protects the original floor from damage.

These decks are available for trucks, vans, El Caminos and Rancheros, and even sport-utility vehicles (SUVs) in wood or aluminum options, giving a stylized and personalized appearance to a modern vehicle. The Retroliner system is a patented full floating-floor system that is clamped in place rather than screwed or bolted into the factory steel or aluminum bed floor. This allows for the custom look and utility of the wood floor while retaining the factory warranty on a new truck. It also creates no diminished resale value if the owner decides to remove the system.

CAD Modeling and the Modern Age of Design

Many custom shops use three-dimensional (3D) design software to develop custom modifications and problem-solving parts. More and more, these shops are using 3D printing in combination with computer-aided design (CAD) modeling to make custom parts in-house and eliminate the cost of

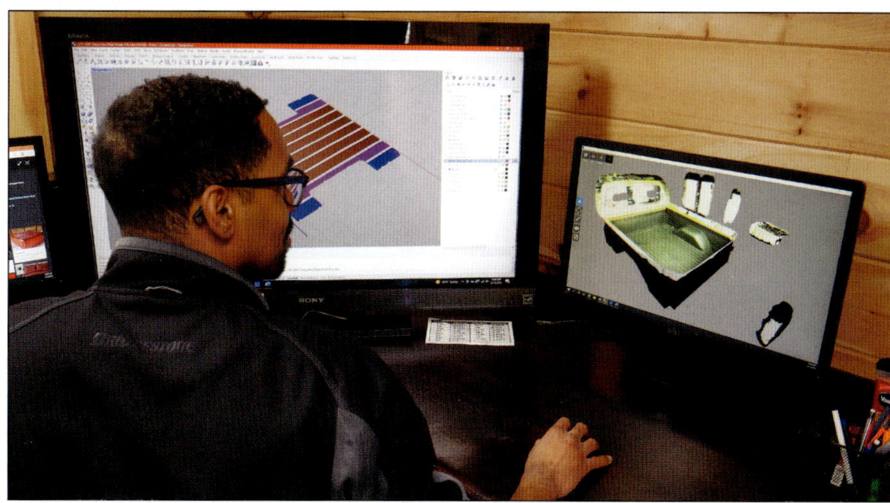

The scans are converted to 3D digital files in CAD software, and the floor is designed for exact tolerances and a perfect fit. These talented designers understand the digital design challenges combined with mass-produced vehicles and the inconsistencies that sometimes occur. (Photo Courtesy Jeff Major/BedWood)

Retroliner floors are available for any truck with a metal floor, including 2022 models. The customer ordering a system can select the type of wood and finish, which then gets pulled and milled into the various pieces of the kit. With the digital modeling and modern milling techniques, turnaround is relatively fast after the order has been made.

The computer-designed files are sent to the CNC cutter table, and the individual boards are made to proper specifications. This automated process is always overseen by a craftsman to ensure that the grain structure, continuity, and integrity of the boards is good as the machine makes precision cuts.

The routing bit edges the boards at the precise angle that will fit the newer bed floors perfectly. Vintage trucks had 90-degree angles at the inner corners, while new trucks utilize gentle-radius curves on inner bed panels. This adds structural integrity and strength to the thinner sheet metal and lightweight aluminum panels in some trucks.

outsourcing one-off custom parts.

The advent and advancement of 3D printed technology has shown amazing growth thanks to the lower cost of equipment and available systems and software to outfit even the smallest shops. Make no mistake, there's still custom work to be done even with computer-designed parts, but the possibilities that open up with the help of computers is nothing short of mind-blowing. Bed-Wood uses 3D scanning technology,

Dozens of finishes are available for any bed wood kit. Any combination can be chosen by the customer, or the floor system can be ordered unfinished. With the huge variety of stain colors, a customer can match the wood color to the vehicle color, depending on the type of wood.

     TRUCK BEDS How to Install, Restore, and Modify

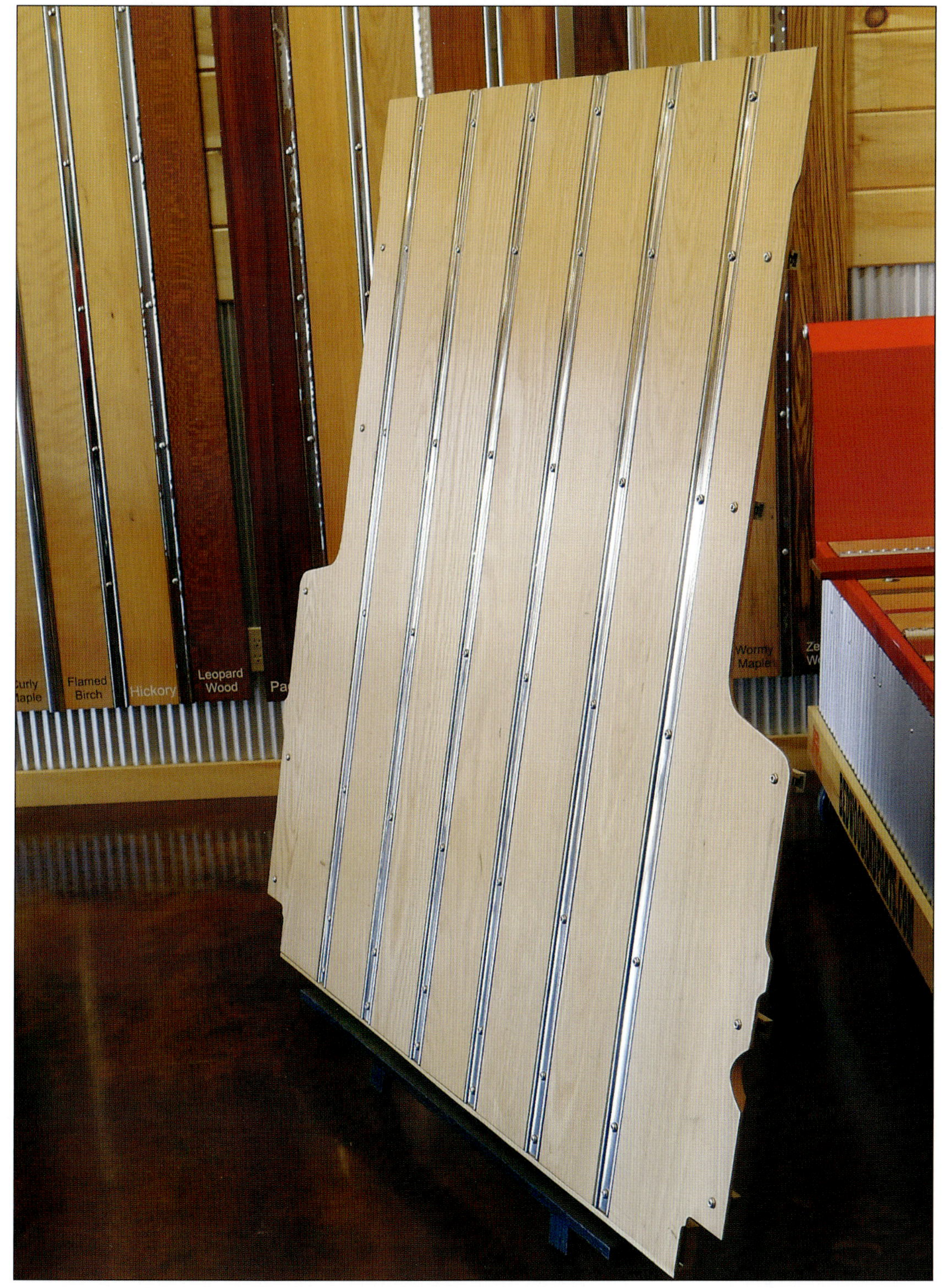

This is a completed kit in a blond finish with a satin polyure-thane clearcoat. It is displayed next to the wood variety and color display in the show-room. This shows how the floor is independent of the vehicle but still is a unit in itself with independent structural integrity.

CAD software, and its wood bed floor production facility to design and manufacture its patented Retroliner systems for most modern trucks and SUVs. Its in-house designers scan and plot out different bed floors and design a floor system that fits perfectly to any vehicle with bed floor space.

Modern computer technology allows many exciting products to be possible. Modern manufacturing techniques, such as CNC (computer numeric control) machining along with CAD software, solve the problem of the many hours it would take to hand fabricate and build parts like this from scratch and also offer

Aluminum cross-braces are lined with a soft rubber pad so that the braces never touch the painted truck bed floor, which would damage the paint. Part of the challenge of designing these systems was to make them easy to install and nondestructive to the original floor.

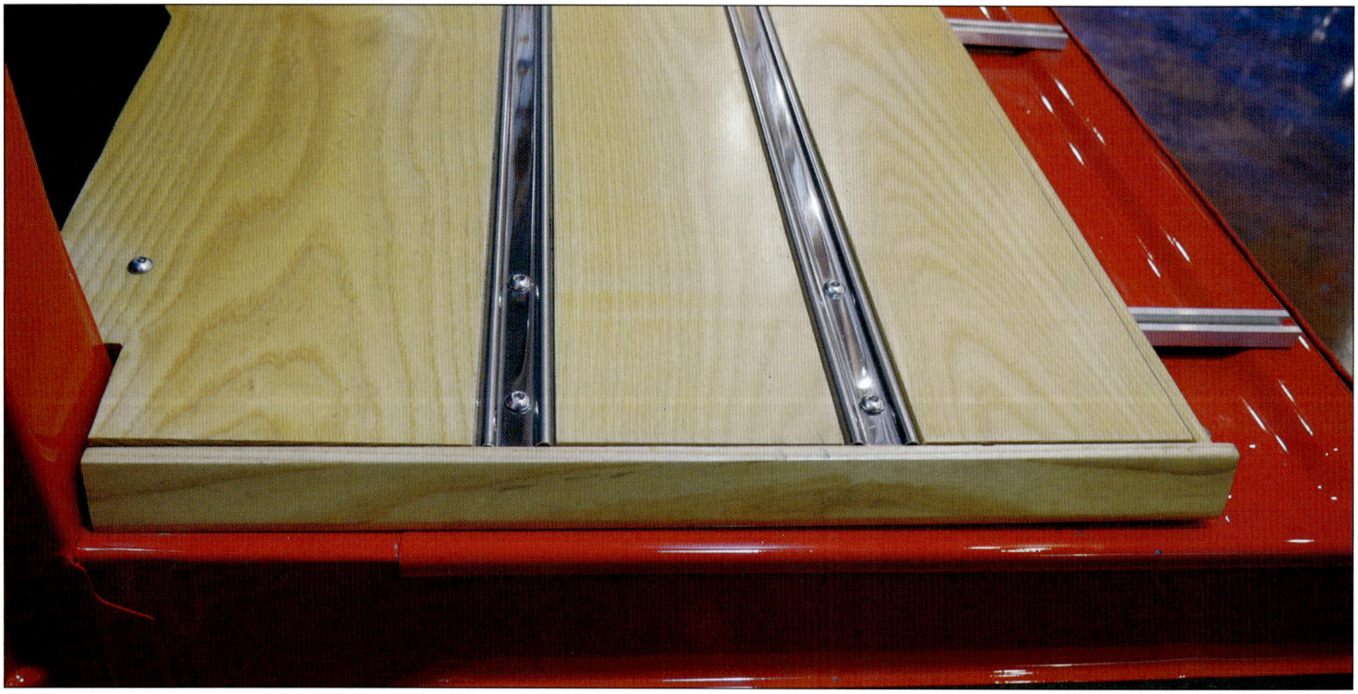

On this cutaway display, the endcap can be seen as well as how it fits to the end of the stainless-steel strips and boards to make an attractive finished edge when the tailgate is opened.

    TRUCK BEDS How to Install, Restore, and Modify

Retroliner is a "floating" floor system, which has a 3/4-inch air gap between most of the floor and the wood. The biggest benefit of this is that moisture won't collect and absorb into or damage the wood or any sheet metal. Water is freely allowed to drain from the bed floor under the wood, much the same as with a drop-in liner or bed-rug system.

The endcap has captured threaded inserts that the hardware can bolt into, which captures the wood planks just like a traditional wood floor in a vintage truck. Instead of it clamping the boards to the truck, the hardware clamps the boards to the substructure of the Retroliner floor.

The cross-supports that are placed every few inches help to distribute the load evenly on the wood floor and onto the metal truck bed to prevent damage. Combined with the soft pad between the aluminum supports, these beds won't initiate vibration damage that miles of driving could produce.

exact repeatability when it comes to manufacturing products in large volume. BedWood is still essentially a sawmill for all intents and purposes, and all the timeless rules and techniques for woodworking still apply, but in concert with today's available technology, companies like this can be extremely prolific.

These amazing tools still don't take the soul out of wood products, since talented craftsmen still must not only conceive and design these products in the first place but also refine and refinish the wood by hand. This creates a modern hybrid of technology and skills that have been passed down and practiced for ages.

The result of this mix of new and old technology is on display. Several different materials are used in construction: wood, of course, but also steel fasteners, aluminum support brackets, and rubber isolators to protect the painted surfaces of the original bed. These liners are floating floors and are held in place by gravity and friction but are non-destructive.

The cost of a new truck today is astronomical, but there's still the possibility of someone cutting the actual floor out of a truck bed to install a vintage kit. I'm sure it's been done by someone somewhere in America, and it would be easy to run a couple of screws down through the wood floor to hold it down tight. However, if you've just invested in a new truck or even leased a new vehicle but still want the style of a wood floor, this is the best solution.

If you've ever leased a vehicle and turned it back in with damage,

This late-model Jeep Gladiator looks great with its floating floor, and the nostalgic wood looks right at home. With the popularity of SUVs, the aftermarket responded with great aftermarket products. Jeeps became an entire subcategory, and with the advent of the Gladiator model, one of the most popular platforms ever produced has become a truck. It's only natural that a wood floor needed to be invented. (Photo Courtesy Jeff Major/BedWood)

Retroliner won the HRIA HPC Best New Product award at the 2014 SEMA Show in the new products showcase. The "retro" exposed fasteners bring nostalgia and a classic look to a modern truck bed floor. This patented design is popular and attractive.

you learn fast that lease contracts penalize you for the smallest amount of damage. There are mileage limits, intense inspections when the vehicle is turned in, and stiff penalties if you've violated any of the clauses in your contract. Imagine turning in a leased truck that has screw holes in eight different places. These systems allow you to customize your truck and not pay penalties.

SUVs with Truck Beds

One of the coolest vehicles in recent years is the Jeep Wrangler JK. The evolution of this platform has been exciting and actually spawned its own aftermarket parts industry. There have been "Day 2" modifications ever since cars have been produced, but Jeep took this to a whole new level.

The vast number of bolt-on aftermarket parts that are accessible for these vehicles is staggering. The Gladiator gave us an actual truck bed in this already truck-ish SUV. It's cool to have a wood deck in the back of a Tahoe or Suburban, but to look over the rails into a Jeep Gladiator is just plain fun.

Along with various wood finishes, BedWood offers laser etching. Email the company a photograph and have it etched into the wood before the finish is applied. This allows personalization, advertise-ment opportunities, and branding options, and it's another way to stylize your bed floor.

This combination of modern technology and traditional wood finishing revolutionized the aftermarket industry (at least in a small way). If you've had the opportunity to attend automotive industry trade shows, such as the Specialty Equipment Marketing Association (SEMA) Show or the Performance Racing Industry Trade Show (PRI), one of the most impressive things that you learn is the vastness of the aftermarket itself.

To be in an inclusive environment comprised of your peers in the industry shows that there's a place for innovation, and there's always room for new products. The industry is made up of hundreds (if not thousands) of small companies that grow into larger and more successful companies. Customizing any vehicle is all about personalizing it and making it your own. There are many ways to do that with any combination of these interesting and attractive bed floor options for any steel-floored or late-model truck, van, or SUV.

This is the bed of a customized and restored vintage E-100 Ford Econoline half-cab truck with a Retroliner floor. The most memorable half cab of all time is the 1960s Dodge A-100 mid-engine wheel-stander known as the Little Red Wagon. There was not much room in the bed on that truck for a wood floor due to a blown Hemi residing there. However, this truck, which was Ford's answer to the A-100 Dodge half-cab truck, benefits from a full wood treatment. These vehicles share the chassis and floors with the vans of the same era, so virtually the same floor that's in this truck would install easily into the van counterpart. It's a cool and versatile option to any vintage or modern vehicle with a metal floor. (Photo Courtesy Jeff Major/BedWood)

CHAPTER 6

CREATING THE ILLUSION OF AGE

The use of patina has been a strong trend in recent years for antique vehicles, either preserving the original character of aged paint or creating the illusion of time-worn panels by using styling and aging methods. Distressed furniture has long been a popular trend, and some of those techniques can be used to create a vintage or aged look to new wood. This way, a truck bed can have the appearance of patina and antique aging but still hold enough structural integrity to work as the manufacturer intended. Preserving patina (or creating "fauxtina") can be fun and rewarding.

It's no secret that I love the look of a handcrafted patina. As a master-certified technician and instructor in collision repair and restoration, I've taken some heat for writing a book on how to create fake patina, but I felt it was important to discuss this as a valid form of customizing. Secondly, there has been a lot of misinformation regarding how to create authentic patina on a vehicle, and because of this, there are less-than-good examples on the streets.

Check out the CarTech title SA447 *Patina: How to Create and Preserve*. It's full of great information and step-by-step instructions.

There are simple rules to follow to create realistic age effects, but there are rules nonetheless. It has been interesting studying how patina is naturally created over time and the chemistry involved between atmosphere and substrate (the air and the surfaces). Clues are all around us as to how things age, and most manmade products are subject to deterioration even when they're meticulously preserved and maintained. All things get old, all surfaces oxidize, and in that is the opportunity to take nature's cues and find a way to apply what naturally occurs to create the illusion of patina.

It's one thing to style the painted sheet metal and trim of a vehicle to look like it's been naturally weathered for a cool custom effect, but it's a whole other ball game to do a faux finish on wood.

Paint is typically layered in micro-thin coats and most time dissimilar colors, so it's quite easy to ether expose applied layers to simulate age or to reapply layers to then distress for an aged effect. Wood, on the other hand, is often left natural, and if there are any coatings, they're thin and often singular, which makes it a little more challenging to patinize. With that being said, with wood, there is so much opportunity to restyle and refinish in dozens of ways with combinations of various techniques.

The amount of distressed furniture that's available in every retail store is a testament to a love of all things vintage, but actually using authentic vintage wood can be problematic. Aged and deteriorated wood crumbles as soon as it's touched. As beautiful as it is, it's really too far gone to serve any purpose other than yard art. It certainly can't be trusted to haul any kind of load.

The challenge when distressing vintage wood is that if it is taken too far, it can affect the integrity of the wood. Achieving a realistic aged effect on new wood is not difficult but requires a different and creative thought process.

Wood finishes delaminate in different ways than painted metal,

This board was purchased from a home center, and it was routed and grooved to fit the center strips of a wood truck bed floor. This board is pine, but any wood with an attractive grain is a great subject.

A rotary tool works well to create wood that looks aged like vintage barn wood. Worn brushes that attach to the tool are used here, but there are many ways to treat the wood to provide a worn appearance.

This technique is provided by TV producer and furniture maker Blaine Seaboalt. The grinder tool can spin upward of 5,000 rpm, which makes this a procedure that demands respect and serious personal protective equipment. I'm using leather gloves, a welding jacket with long sleeves, safety glasses, a plastic shield, and a lot of care. The wire wheel has a habit of launching broken wire fragments, so be careful if you try this on your project.

The wire wheel removes soft portions of the grain and leaves the harder layers raised, creating the depth that aged wood usually has after years of exposure. I'm using a sharp awl to poke holes into the surface to simulate worm holes.

Let the spinning tool slowly glide over the top surface of the wood in the direction of the grain or in a linear direction on the board. Using this tool across the grain destroys the grain instead of exposing it.

and unfinished wood surfaces (such as vintage truck beds) are much more susceptible to whatever's been dumped into or hauled on them throughout the years. I will provide some simple techniques to change the appearance of fresh, new wood into an aged surface, but the truth is that it can be a lot of fun to just experiment and figure out what "fauxtina" you want to create.

Creating Patina on New Wood

Many styling techniques have been developed by the motion picture industry over the years, creating sets and backdrops for various films. Prop stylists are not so inclined to give away

TRUCK BEDS How to Install, Restore, and Modify

Any hard tool works for this effect, but the claw side of a hammer can be used to dig gauges in the surface to simulate years of abuse and loads that may have been carelessly tossed into the bed. Remember, you're telling a story. The story can be anything you want, but you want clues of authenticity and realism.

all of their secrets, but with the advent of social media and video sites, some people that share their techniques and are willing to teach how they arrived at a certain finish.

What do green tea, claw hammers, wire wheels, and grinders have in common? Usually, nothing. However, in our case, they're all involved in creating a very authentic barnwood effect on a very inexpensive piece of pine purchased from the home center. The cost of a complete replacement bed kit hovers around $1,000, and kits with exotic wood can go much higher. The money-saving opportunity alone should nudge you toward learning about a cool custom floor.

Even if you're not inclined to fauxtina your truck bed floor, these techniques can be used on furniture, wall boards, crown molding, or benchtops if you want a vintage look to your workshop. The topcoats that I use are different in chemistry and appearance, but both offer a high level of protection while enhancing the appearance. This creates a functional element to what is essentially a piece of art.

After distressing the plank to the desired effect, make a thick paste with a mixture of organic green tea powder and tap water. The green tea activates tannins in the wood and creates a contrast over the various densities of the wood, providing an aged look. The consistency of pancake batter works well for your mixture.

Use a shop towel to rub the mixture into the wood grain. However, an old T-shirt will also work—or just about anything that absorbs water. Work the solution into the grain of the wood so that none of the unstained wood is visible. Once it is rubbed in, remove most of the excess with a clean towel. A certain amount of the mix stays in the porous wood and provides a nice contrast after a brief wipe down.

Let the board dry overnight to make sure any moisture has evaporated. Then, brush on a coat of clear satin polyurethane. Make sure that you seal the back side, front and back end-grains, and deep into any recesses to keep out moisture.

Follow the manufacturers recommendations on recoating. However, you should have a second coat on the top surfaces for strength. This manufacturer says to recoat between 4 to 6 hours and lightly sand between coats. I didn't sand between coats because it may have diminished the rough look. Let it dry for at least 24 hours before reassembly or use.

Personalizing Your Patina

The fun aspect about this is that there's almost no point at which you can't recover from experimenting. I use nails, screwdrivers, hammers, wire wheels, and green tea to arrive at a very weathered look that's quite authentic. The damage that you can do to a piece of wood with a wire wheel on a 5/8-inch arbor grinder is astounding. This machine used to serve as a polisher many years ago, but now it's relegated to stripping duties on sheet-metal or

The finished barn-wood board looks great! The subtle character can be seen in the wood, and it has a genuine aged appearance. It would take about 10 to 12 hours to do an entire wood floor, which is actually much faster than a traditional smooth-stain and polyurethane finish.

projects like this wood plank. With the 7-pound weight of the machine itself multiplied by the ridiculous RPMs, you can move a lot of wood. So, be careful and use appropriate safety gear.

Aged wood has a distinctively darker tone than fresh-cut wood. Being a porous organic material, wood is absorbent and holds onto all kinds of discoloring contamination and debris, all of which give it the barnwood character that I aim to achieve with this sample. The green tea activates tannins in the wood and provides a contrast to the softer pulp next to the hard grains that get exposed with the wire wheel. Leaving it alone is an interesting look, but the green coloration is not what I'm after here, so a coating of polyurethane will do two jobs.

Two coats of satin polyurethane seal out moisture and protect the wood to a degree, but it also immediately eliminates the green overtone and turns brown. A gloss polyurethane would also have a very different look, much like a shellac, which can be attractive. I really wanted the satin look on this sample, since the lack of gloss alludes to an older coating.

I always advocate, whether it's on a car panel or a wood project, to do a practice or sample board to determine a strategy. It's a time investment that teaches you how to create repeatable results and, frankly, is therapeutic. The time to experiment is not on your actual project! For the two hours and $10 dollars that it took to buy the wood and materials to create a sample, it's well worth the investment. If you're doing this for a client or customer, this also serves as a sample to get approval for a job moving forward.

Driftwood

If you've ever walked along a riverbank or ocean beach and seen driftwood, you know it can be truly beautiful. Nature's brush has all the tones and more. To see the subtle nuance of natural age is not only something to appreciate but also to use as an example regarding how to make something appear older than it really is.

Weather Wash stain is a water-based product that activates wood tannins. The company offers several tones as well as other products, such as gloss and satin clear finishes. The oak color, when used on the pine sample, has a very light gray tone and a distinctive driftwood look. These products are active stains and need to have exposed tannins in wood to create the illusion of age. This means that they must be sanded or abraded to activate tannins and allow penetration into the wood pulp. Without this, the stain itself cannot be absorbed, and the effect is greatly diminished.

Weather Wash recommends sanding with 60- to 80-grit sandpaper to open the grain. I accomplished this with 80-grit sandpaper while routing the boards in Chapter 2. Used on oak or a darker wood, these water-based stains take on different overtones and can add dimension to the most boring piece of raw timber. However, these products must be used on unfinished

Another great way to get a weathered look without sacrificing the strength of the wood is with a Weather Wash finish. Several tones can be achieved with this water-based stain, and the various stains can be combined to create a unique effect. This non-toxic product works with the tannins in the wood in a non-destructive way and creates a nice weathered look very quickly.

This is the result after two coats that were at least an hour apart. The grain is nicely pronounced, and the gray tone is perfect. This could be left as it is, but the stain provides no protection from moisture or any impact, so use a compatible clear protective coat. Let it dry overnight before moving to the next step.

and properly prepped wood only. Lighter woods generally have less tannin content, and darker wood has a higher concentration.

Tannin in timber is a naturally occurring chemical that assists in the protection of the wood, mostly by hindering insects and minimiz-ing damage from them. Tannins in wine are what make a "dry" wine feel dry. This type of a stain, since it's water based, works extremely fast due to the porosity of the wood and soaks into the grain quickly.

This type of stain is interesting because of the unpredictability of the reaction and overall color. No two pieces of wood are identical, and this type of active stain accentu-ates that effect. It creates a random and unpredictable outcome that is different than a solvent-based stain, which tends to coat over the wood evenly. Active stains provide a natural-looking effect.

Water-Based and Oil-Based Clear Coatings

It may seem like you shouldn't use oil-based finish coats on top of a water-based product, but that's not the case. As long as you allow the water-based stain to fully cure (which can be 60-to-90 days), you can make the two types of coatings adhere to each other.

This oak color provides a sun-bleached driftwood look. Use a foam brush and wipe the stain in the direction of the grain. This product is water-thin, so be aware of splashing and dripping onto the tabletop or floor. Even though it's a water-based product, use gloves to protect your skin.

TRUCK BEDS How to Install, Restore, and Modify

Once curing has completed on the water-based stain, lightly abrade the surface with a 150-grit screen (or an equivalent scuffing pad), being careful not to remove too much of the stain. You're creating tiny scratches in the surface for the oil-based topcoat to cling to (it's like Velcro on a microscopic scale).

It's much easier, however, to simply use a compatible water-based polyurethane finish coat while you're within the crosslink window of the stain. You can apply up to four coats for a very durable coating. If desired, you can sand and reapply after the first 4 coats have fully cured. This can create somewhat of a bar-top appearance, where any grain of the wood is completely buried under the polyurethane.

Lightly sand between coats with 320-grit sandpaper and a soft block. This technique smooths the surface so that the next coat lays down very flat. If you were layering up the finish, you can sand between every second or third coat. As long as you let the finish cure between sanding, you can create the effect you want. Water-based finishes are extremely durable out in the elements, and this technology is used more and more for home construction and refinishing due to the minimal toxicity and environmentally friendly disposal.

If your goal is to have your wood floor installed and functional quickly, a fauxtina finish may be exactly what you need. There's craftsmanship and art involved in any woodworking project, and those disciplines demand respect.

However, enjoying your project and creating a centerpiece for conversations at a car show is a great reason to choose a finish that takes much less time. It's also a way to get out of your garage much sooner than the time it takes to refinish a wood bed floor kit in a traditional manner.

There's beauty in the roughness and how age-styling a truck's wood bed floor is something that can be done with simple tools in a short amount of time. Also, it's a bonus that it can be done on a frugal budget.

Make the first application as a full but conservative coat, and allow it to dry for at least four hours before lightly sanding out any imperfections.

Using 320-grit sandpaper on a soft face sanding block, dry sand the surface only enough to smooth any dust or debris flat.

Apply two coats of a waterborne satin polyurethane coating. This particular coating is non-yellowing and darkens the stain much less than a conventional solvent-borne topcoat. It's also very clear and doesn't have the yellowish look of a conventional polyurethane, which is why I chose it. I wanted the gray overtones to stay.

Lightly sand in the direction of the grain, which is a good habit to get into on any project. Sanding across the grain disturbs the natural pattern and could possibly create distracting scratches that may show through the topcoat.

Before the second coat is applied, gently wipe off the dust from the surface with a damp cloth. This removes any debris that could mix with the next coat and show through as contamination or rough spots in the finish.

Using a foam brush, apply another flow-coat that is heavier than the first one but not flooded on. Make sure to seal the end-grain and back side of any wood floor project to reduce moisture penetration and damage.

After drying overnight, the finish looks smooth, and the satin sheen is even. A cured waterborne finish is every bit as strong as a cured solvent finish. The added bonus is that it doesn't affect the final color of the stain and provides a true driftwood color.

The distressed wood finish, when fully cured, looks amazingly authentic. With the unrestored painted bed strip installed, the illusion of age is complete, but the integrity and ability to still handle a load is still intact.